The Last Teardrop

G. Antoinette George

The Last Teardrop

ISBN: 1-59352-252-5

Published by:
Christian Services Network
833 Broadway, Suite #201
El Cajon, CA 92021
Toll Free: 1-866-484-6184
www.CSNbooks.com

Coming soon, Book #2 – *Single And Celibate.*

Also, coming soon, Book #3 – *Extreme Betrayal.*

Printed in the United States of America.

DEDICATION

This book is dedicated to Georgette Morgan, my sister/daughter.

I AFFIRM YOU THIS DAY!

Table of Contents

INTRODUCTION

Can you imagine a world with perfect parents who give birth to perfect babies and then, with great perfection, raise up these perfect babies into perfect adulthood?

Can you imagine a world with imperfect parents who give birth to perfect babies, only to fail at nurturing and protecting these perfect babies entrusted to their care? Have you wondered why some people are burdened with such awful loads in early childhood? Do you ask, "Where is God?" as it seems they are born with an unfathomable lot. Many children become victims of their surroundings, while others become victors. Why is this? Are ill-fated beginnings destined to become the starting point for immense sorrow throughout life? Is it destiny when wretched and shameful beginnings evolve into magnificence?

When Ms. George asked me to edit *The Last Teardrop*, I felt vastly unequipped to handle such a task, yet a discord in my soul led me to acquiescence as her obedience to God in seeking my help became increasingly plain.

The Last Teardrop, is an exhilarating story of life. It is not uncommon to learn of news accounts depicting young defenseless children who are abused, sexually assaulted, and/or murdered by society's deviants. For the boys and girls who survive, rarely is their outcome publicized. Unfortunately, we simply forget about abused and hurting children; victims left to wonder, or forget the adjustments society's children must make as they cope with the worst kind of atrocities any defenseless boy or girl should endure. A tale of having one's heart ripped out and then healed and a sad spirit restored takes the reader on a true account of Glenda's not-so-nice life. A paradox of secrets, repressed memories, blithe defiance to a tattered marriage and betrayals unveiled in the story of an abused child, later woman, who confronted the "victim" odds and chose instead to become the victor.

Though we have never met, Glenda is my friend, my sister. It is my belief our circle of friendship will expand exponentially as you sojourn this winding path through her pain and ultimate jubilation. You will not simply read this manuscript; rather you journey vicariously through every unfettered thought. Warning, her walk may become difficult for those who live in denial of the harsh reality that a walk with God does not perfect you. Or, if you see the world through dark-colored glasses to blind yourself from the impact of all-too-familiar evil acts upon society's children and choose to do nothing; it is not easy. For those who seek healing from similar atrocities, my friend will reach mightily for your hand, enjoining you to become her friend and climb again up this mountain.

Thank you, my friend and sister, for trusting me to accompany you on this leg of your journey. A journey meant to entwine our lives, and now we walk together in leading the way for hurting women, and men, to find healing, restoration, and joy.

> *For I know the plans I have for you, says the Lord. Plans for good and not for evil, to give you a future and a hope.*
>
> (Jeremiah 29:11 KJV)

Acknowledgements

Mother Divine,

You gently but firmly guided me back into your womb for wholeness. The path to your heart seemed never ending, and oh so painful. Like a fierce mother, You pulled me into rest unaware of my own tiredness. How exhausting is such insensitivity to one's self? You encouraged me to rest when I was tired, but gently kept nudging me along.

My Stepfather, My Dad, Mr. Studley Joseph

Growing up I thought, "He is perfectly strange." You would whip my butt when I got out of line. You did not treat me as other men did; instead, you gazed upon your daughter with great love. When your eyes turned my way, love held me tighter each time. You became God's witness of a father. Thank you, Uncle Joe.

My Family

I owe you so much. Like the world, you are reading for the first time the live, unfolding of my journey to the Mother Divine's heart. You will now experience the internal hell, the chaos, my tears, my fears, and anger without having the comprehension of what was and why it had to happen to your daughter, sister, niece, cousin, or friend. Some of you will glean an understanding, may experience guilt…as perhaps you knew and helplessly stood by motionless. Regardless, a journey of unknown destination, but rooted in trust in an Almighty God who held a plan for my deliverance: You will marvel at the love from which these words emanate. I love you, George, Kerry, and baby Kemyoe.

Janice Guider, My Friend, My Editor

You are certainly one of a kind. Your integrity, your honesty, your obedience to the Holy Spirit of God within you is so very rare. You became a friend, a true friend to me before you became my editor. I would not trade you for the world. You became a voice in the gloom during the darkest season of this journey. Your voice guided me when I could not see. I thank you for being true to God, and true to yourself. You are indeed a sister divine. I love you.

My Sister

Such a beautiful sister, Gillian Richards, who read while I wrote. You never regretted you had an email address (I think). You bore the pain of this journey with me, and never showed frustration, but listened with the silence I needed. Thank you for your heart.

Kathy Spaar

My Spiritual Director, you had the most unique responsibility of keeping me focused and on the path. I hear you saying, "There is a divine purpose for you, dear." May you be at peace, may your heart remain open, may you awaken to the light of your own true nature, may you be healed, and may you be a source of healing for all beings." Thank you, Kathy.

My best friend Blondell Baltimore

You are the best and truest friend any woman on a journey could ask for. Like my family you had no idea what I was going through. Yet, you allowed me to disappear in silence for weeks, and never condemned or made me feel guilty when I returned. You offered me your unconditional love and your wadadli style cooking. You are indeed my sister divine. You are my friend.

Marie Pinto

You are my sister/friend/psychotherapist. You helped me peer through the muddy walls of my darkened memory. I would not have dared to do this without you. Thank you so much. I love you.

Mayor of Jersey City (*former and soon to become again*) Mayor L. Harvey Smith

You are one in a million. You possess the heart of a lamb, clothed in the layer of a lion. You are God's chosen man for this generation. Be still and know that He is God.

Mrs. Alice Slaughter

You were there for my family, when we had no other. You allowed our tears to fall on your shoulder. You are indeed a mother.

Bishop Mayes

You are a spiritual father and mentor. Hold to God's unchanging hand. You are indeed an example of how one can live in this world, and yet not be of this world. You are an example of who God is. I **adore you.**

G. Antoinette George

The Last Teardrop

My story of the journey to the Feminine Divine, my Mother

Know this, as with you, the comfortless, and me …

All that was set in motion when my mother's womb held me

Until this moment,

As the arms of our Father Divine, hold me this day.

All that came from heaven and hell, yes even hell,

Has prepared me for this moment.

Being pressed to bring comfort to a hurting people.

G. Antoinette George

Chapter One

Weep

For his wrath is only for a minute; in his grace there is life; weeping may be for a night, but joy comes in the morning.

(Psalm 30:5, BBE)

Weeping has endured for 41 years, where is joy? Morning has come and gone, but joy did not come. Or has she?

March 10, 2005...and it is ten minutes after 6 o'clock in the morning.

I am still, muted, quiet as commanded. Worshipping in the spirit as I kneel in the presence of the Lord. Real holy, right in his presence. Suddenly, the question I had been asking the Holy Spirit for over a year came with force to my mind, "Who am I?"

The forceful reply that crippled my already dead comfortless soul, "You are a prostitute." Shame and depression overtake me. Depression, I'm told is the other side of anger or anger turned inside out.

The voice seemed to come from a well-kept journal.

Comfort, I am comfortless at this moment.

He named up to 22 sexual assaults by the time I was 15 years old.

Each one raping me, stealing from me, robbing me, molesting me endlessly, so it seemed. Extreme betrayal of innocence assaults my childlike trust with detached sinfulness, then and now.

Even now.

Repulsive and lasting suffering in the face of Comfort: Suffering hurts.

I jumped up from my knees, no longer feeling very holy, and armed in full rebellion, yelled, "You have got to be kidding." Rather speedily, I abandoned my hallowed area of worship. Sacred pain. Like David, I was astonished with silence; I held my peace, as sorrow stirred in the depths of my soul. He had better be kidding.

He was not. "Comfort my people."

My childhood had not been safe and perfect, as I had imagined. My only complaint, until this recent revelation, was that I grew up with a mentally ill mother as my guardian...the assigned protector and nurturer of my soul. My life entrusted to this woman, my mother. Why not?

Nevertheless, life abounded as I matured: Married into a pressure cooker marriage for over twenty-two years. Blessed with two wonderful children. Blessed with a gift of returning to God workmanship rewarded with a great business; with the gift of being a doer. Hey! The loneliness, fear, shame and pain had mysteriously channeled itself into positive outcomes for me. Yes, I know I am an overcomer, not because of any of the aforementioned accomplishments, though thankful for them: I am an overcomer because as much as the demons tried to steal my life, kill me and destroy me forever, Satan was not allowed to complete his plan. That's a child who overcame.

I whisper to You, Great Comforter ...

Talking 'bout a child, who do love Jesus;
Here's one; here's one.
Talking 'bout a child, who do love Jesus,
Here's one; here's one.
Talking 'bout a child who's been buked and scorn,
Talking 'bout a child with a soul that's worn;

Talking 'bout a child, who do love Jesus,
Here's one. Here's one.[1]

But now, let's get this straight, you are telling me I was indeed wrought by the violence of rape, molestation, betrayal, abandonment, shame and mental illness? Such misfortune served me and is now part of the reason for this momentous journey, on my bike and under a cloud of rain.

Are You sure it's the correct route, Elijah?

This is Antoinette, Miss Pure, Miss Perfection, and Miss Holy according to me and I am quite serious.

You must be kidding.

<u>March 13, 2005</u> and it is five fifty-six in the evening.

Okay, You are not kidding.

It is true.

I need to understand why. I don't just need to understand, I am mad as hell. Where were You? What did You say? You were at the end of my journey? The beginning?

Ha!

Where, who, and at what age did it begin?

"Extreme betrayal requires extreme forgiveness. Being betrayed is bad enough, becoming bitter is a defeat you cannot afford."

"Got it," I replied, remembering quite honestly that we are not at the end of this journey yet.

[1]Negro Spiritual

Repressed memories.

So, what happened?

How old was I?

I need to know.

I need to understand.

Who betrayed me?

Where the hell was my mother?

Why did You allow it, Jesus?

Why twenty-two sexual assaults by my fifteenth birthday; each one raping or molesting, violating me several times over. Why twenty-two? Why not one or two? Why twenty-two?

Did You turn Your back on me Jesus? You gave me life through a mother possessed by a god-awful demon of mental illness.

My head hurts so badly. If it exploded right now, would everyone think I'm mentally ill? Do I dare begin to believe my birthright now becomes the cross I bear; I share with my mother all over again? I am trying to hold it together here, Comfort, so just jump in anytime.

No!

You removed Your protection so the devil could do any thing to me except kill me?

Why? Why do I get to live through this hell? Perhaps death would have been kinder?

Don't You think so?

Was this kind of abuse necessary for Your purpose?

You said Satan could do nothing without Your authorization. I had no one but You. Everywhere I went, everyone I turned to, ended up hurting me; and yet You constantly tell me, **I AM**...You are in control.

"Antoinette, I will not speak unless you are still. You cannot speak and listen at the same time. Remember, my condition is stillness. I will show you Your Father's plan for your life."

After all the hell I have been through, He'd better have a plan.

"I will ignore that remark, Antoinette. Do not be like a horse or a mule, whose mouth must be held in with a bridle."

March 19, 2005

Comfort, did I fall asleep?

I had a strange dream. In the dream, my family and I were dressing to attend church. In illusive harmony, everyone was getting dressed. A little girl appeared busily sweeping the floor. She looked and felt like my daughter. She kept whispering to me as she cleaned, but her voice was so soft, I barely understood her.

I said to her, "Honey, for mommy to understand what you are saying, you have to stand still and speak louder." She repeated to me what she needed. A stranger had stopped by earlier and brought our family some treats; she wanted what she thought belonged to her.

"Antoinette, you have met your daughter. Your daughter is you. She will relive your life's journey with you."

"Comfort, she is so beautiful, so soft spoken and always sweeping. She is so small to be four years old, little more than a toddler. She has to be younger than four. How old is she?"

"She'll be with you on this journey, ask her age."

I sure will. I am so anxious to meet her again. I want to hug her, love her, and just hold onto her. I love her so much already. She wanted some treats, but incessantly kept on sweeping the floor, her busyness made it impossible to share anything with this precious child.

"Antoinette, don't be anxious. This stage of the journey cannot be rushed. This is an extremely delicate season that involves much pain." When memory returns with her pain, it is more painful than the actual event. Let her reveal your journey slowly. Take your time with each incident, because she will have grown a little older each time you meet her."

"So, after each revelation and the pain of it, enjoy her for some time." She is the daughter you always wished you had, that you do have. Don't rush, take your time, and live through every moment."

Okay, Comfort.

<u>April 03, 2004</u>, I had a dream.

In this dream I traveled on a familiar highway toward home. However, my home in the dream was located in New York. I actually reside in New Jersey. Traveling a highway that would take me directly home, I soon came to recognize I was on the wrong side of the highway. Even though either direction of the highway would ultimately lead me home, one road had more difficulty and numerous detours. Soon, it dawned on me; this chosen path increasingly carried me into a more difficult course. It seemed my fate was to stay this course, while unsure why I was being led down this path.

Such a choice ultimately brought me to the end of the highway, leaving me now in a very unfamiliar town. The rain fell profusely. The soil in the town, as far as my eye could see, was a rich, dark brown mud.

Standing in the middle of the town, the rain only covered me. (Go figure) It was as though I'd been assigned a personal cloud. There were women, men, and children sitting and standing all around. Could they see me?

Suddenly, I was riding a bike. Almost magically, my mode of transportation became two wheels and would only move when I pedaled.

The town's people stood in line to speak to the Evangelist, who had come to their town for a crusade. I imagined they wanted prayers as he sat in a booth, along with his followers. The rain did not touch any of them and I wondered if I had become invisible.

I pedaled over to one of the tables, and asked a man for help. Before the man could answer, a woman walking by answered, "You were on the easy road, and you got off here?" She laughed and walked away. Confused by her demeanor, but more relieved to know physically, I'm not blocked out. Abruptly the dream ended with no understanding for me. I did not understand, neither could I shake the effects of the dream from my thoughts.

A Sabbath Keeping

An inventory of my past revealed there was nothing I felt worthy of sharing. Shame would put me in a chokehold of the real truth: Too many betrayals, fear, rejection, adultery, lies, anger, mental Illness, molestation, and sexual abuse. Fertilizer thriving within the vacuum of a seemingly perfect family: A Sabbath keeping, go to church three times a week, gospel singing, we clap our hands and sway to the music and go on as a family.

Even as a young girl I grew totally disgusted and confused by the hypocrisy. A word foreign to me during those early days when even as a child sucked into this vacuum, I heard a still small voice whispering, "Comfort my people." I think, "Comfort my people? You comfort me."

My pain, hazy to those surrounding me, began its search for a place to hide. It needed rest. I had tremendous inward pain and anger.

Not unlike you, I dream. Perhaps, unlike you the dreams became the energy that led to the hiding place where all that pain hid itself for years.

On April 5, 2004, I spent the entire day in worship.

It was during that time that the Holy Spirit whispered to me, "Comfort my people." "A soul that is dead cannot bring life," I replied. What exactly was the Holy Spirit talking about? I pondered comfort.

To give strength and hope to.

To ease the grief or trouble of.

Okay, God understands comfort. Is this just like God to use me as a tool to bring comfort to others even as I felt comfortless? He says, "But I have chosen you to bring comfort to my people."

All that might have brought me comfort and security in life was snatched away.

So, God, how will I recognize comfort and know I was walking in obedience locked into this place of great discomfort for me? Does Comfort truly know me? Am I losing my mind? What would Comfort look like, feel like, act like?

Mindful that in the dream, I chose to stay this course. Or did this course draft me? This journey seemed new, and instinctively I felt an unfamiliar discomfort though peaceful that God would travel with me on this new journey. A journey I was not quite prepared to participate in, for instinctively I knew the revelation in the dream was a path along a long, dusty road. Rain would constantly fall upon me; for how long, I was clueless.

Comfort lies and waits behind the worst fear, betrayal, shame and adultery the human mind can conceive. I really wish Comfort would take her place before the homes of betrayal, shame, abandonment, molestation, and rape.

Such demons boldly thrive in the city, they flourish in the cesspool of business and coldness in an urban wilderness: a wilderness of quicksand pulling apart the heart of the family; pulling at the existence of humankind. Would we have to change our address, move to the suburbs to find comfort? In the appearance of Comfort, the demons can hide more easily. Secrets find more places to hide along the tree-lined streets and lanes of material comfort of your journey. There is no comfort in secrets.

Still, why me?

Sometimes, I feel like a motherless child;
Sometimes, I feel like a motherless child;
Sometimes, I feel like a motherless child,
A long way from home, from home.
A long way from home.

Still, why me? I am so unworthy.

Why at a time when I am so tired, abandoned by those who should love me effortlessly, washed up, fed-up and stilled now by mental anguish warring against my flesh? My mind is like jelly.

After all the hell you have been through, She can't usher you into her presence, until you are still.

Still, with a beast burning in my stomach.

Still, uttering no sound.

Subdued by a self-imposed, deafening silence as the revelations become more clear and real.

Okay, Comfort, to be still, I have to listen to my body. May I listen to my body? Do You hear the cries of my soul? Thus far the journey from what I am beginning to remember, the journey to You was so cruel and void of love.

May I listen to my body and embrace the brokenness again without letting You go; without blaming You and jeopardizing the trust I have found in You? Will You embrace me, Comfort, and hold me through this terrible ordeal?

Can't we compromise?

Help me to understand this total stillness business. Please.

I would have to live through the brokenness again and no matter how painful, still I trust You.

For me, Your favorite daughter, could we ignore still? Please.

Okay, so You are only effective when I am still. Here goes, I will be still as my soul is opened for the journey. It might be too much for You, Comfort, but this is Your condition.

I was born on February 04, 1964, the daughter of Menelice Allen and Clarence George. Born in Antigua, a small island in the Caribbean, I don't know if I entered this world in a hospital or at home. Regardless, I made it in. My mother's pride and joy *maybe*. The delight of my father's heart: Certainly not my earthly dad. I have no memory of his presence. My maternal grandmother, passed from this life when I was about four years old. How did she die? I don't know. Did I kill her? I don't think so. I have a single memory of the woman; she was lying in a box. There is no recollection of her before her death or after her demise. One solitude memory, she was in a box.

So, I am four years old, and starting to feel rather special. Nice little curves coming together. But listen to this, Comfort, I was not the only one thinking I am special.

Why at four did I notice the curves? Am I allowed to ask questions?

The first of over twenty adult men thought I was rather special also. Keep in mind, Comfort, this memory of the first season of my life was gone until now. Even the pain abandoned me! How does a mind and soul lock out such pain without the mercy of Comfort? You were there, weren't You? The loss of memory kept me sane. There was no other way I could have endured the traumas of the second season of this path with these new revelations.

I am telling You of my journey as it is being revealed to me. So bear with me. Allow me to cry. Allow me to be broken. Allow me anger, You and I must see what I went through together. But You know already, don't You, Comfort? You were there all the time and blocked the memory of these vile acts on this defenseless little girl to help me survive such atrocities. You kept me alive.

For the redemptive work of the cross to take place, the spirit of Elijah must first come. To be honest with You, Comfort, the Spirit of Elijah hurts. I really did not like him. He keeps digging and digging, looking for a root. My root was just fine. I am a God-fearing, gospel singing, abused, but proper child of God. The root was solid.

I started to become really agitated with this Spirit of Elijah, because as he moves closer to the root he speaks: "extreme betrayal requires extreme forgiveness." What is he talking about?

And, why am I scared? What can hurt me now? The shame those evil men forced on me? Why should I feel more shame than they when I was the child, defenseless and torn up by their wickedness? Can my mother's mental illness hurt me still, even though she is dead? Or perhaps the revelation of the extreme forgiveness has not come for me yet?

This might give You a really good laugh Comfort, this is what he replied,

"The spirit of Elijah is not sadness, the spirit of Elijah is repentance, repentance is change, and change is joy."

You go figure.

Anyway, I am thinking, let's get this over with, because He claims His job isn't done until He gets to the root.

But Comfort, even as I planned my objection and of course denial, I felt the painful pull of the root. So, it's really my root. It's profoundly deep but the hardened dirt is suddenly loose and being washed away. Things are coming to the surface.

My God!

My holy response, "Whatever the reasons, Lord, use it for Your name, honor, and glory."

Even while saying that to the Lord, I am thinking, Is He for real?

He knew I was going to grow up and love Him, and this is the best He could do? He has got to be kidding, a virtuous daughter indeed.

CHAPTER TWO

Special Directions

BEING PRESSED INTO SERVICE

Jeremiah 18:1-8

This is the word that came to Jeremiah from the LORD: "Go down to the potter's house, and there I will give you my message." So I went down to the potter's house, and I saw him working at the wheel. But the pot he was shaping from the clay was marred in his hands; so the potter formed it into another pot, shaping it as seemed best to him. Then the word of the LORD came to me: "O house of Israel, can I not do with you as this potter does?" declares the LORD. "Like clay in the hand of the potter, so are you in my hand, O house of Israel. If at any time I announce that a nation or kingdom is to be uprooted, torn down and destroyed, and if that nation I warned repents of its evil, then I will relent and not inflict on it the disaster I had planned.

"Your life is a symbol of the life of the Black Nation."

"Your Spirit and your faith in your Father is so strong, all of Satan's attacks had to be concentrated."

"Every evil act, every attempt against your life, concentrated."

"Yet you kept rising."

"Most would have died from the abuse, but you kept rising."

"Your spirit represents the spirit of the Black Nation."

"Satan had no weapon that was strong enough to keep them down."

"Their spirit is like cured yeast, it kept rising under my conditions."

"You were chosen and sent here to bring your people out."

"They shall rise, and this time they will remain standing."

"You are the Baton that I have raised."

"You have been raised as a personal confirmation of my covenant with your people."

"A nation will live because you chose life."

"You will be a light to guide all nations to me."

Okay, Comfort, I am kinda starting to understand.

As I tell You the stories, explain to me why they were necessary.

(Can You stop the rain though? Or is the rain making me more pliable for You, the Potter, to change me?) Help me to understand the rain.

I remember, I was about 4 years old. Just before I go any farther I think I need a little help to relate my life.

Thoughts ...

- "Psychotherapy and Spirituality go together."
- "A spiritual purpose for my psychotic life."
- "You led me to a place called Sanctuary in Beallsville, Maryland."
- "Never heard of it before, but You said You would be there to meet me."
- "You said I would be provided a safe vacuum in peace, quiet and tranquility."

Okay, so here I am at Sanctuary. Barbara, the Ministry Director, suggested I wait until I am settled into this vacuum before continuing my story. While I am settling in, Kathy, Your spiritual director is telling me how safe You are, how You want to nurture me. She said You have placed a light around me.

Is this true?

Oh yes, I feel it. I feel the light. I can see it. The violet flame.

Kathy is a Roman Catholic and white, and she is your usher? Appointed to lead me into the presence of the Feminine Divine, and brings Your joy and direction particularly to all Your daughters.

"Antoinette, I don't see color or religious denominations, I created color and change...purposely creating differences in mankind. When I look at my children, I see the heart. I see my Son's blood. Kathy has a heart of flesh. Her heart is broken and contrite before me. She is my usher chosen to escort you into Comfort's presence. I am a God of beauty. Beauty comes in a variety of colors. Wouldn't it be boring if all the flowers were one color? All the trees bore the same fruits? How dreary that would become? So this is what I did, I covered the souls in different colors of clothing of flesh. She was tried in the fire, and came out gold. You were tried in the fire, and came out gold. Looks the same to me."

"Namaste, the Divine in you has met the Divine in her.

"She is your sister."

Okay, back to my life's journey.

I am sitting in counsel with Marie Pinto, the psychotherapist in the real world that Barbara recommended. I am beginning to remember and it hurts. This extreme betrayal hurts. I was only about 4 years old. I am at home, where I lived with my mother, grandmother and a family friend.

PRINCESS

Oh, Comfort, let me just sit here for a while.

I am so weak.

I think I have a fever.

I saw her again.

My daughter.

Me.

She said her name is Antoinette, but every one says her Daddy calls her princess.

She is definitely younger than 4 years old.

I don't quite understand why I am recording all this information. I really need to be someplace else, having myself a well-deserved pity party. But nooooo, Antoinette, has to keep the broom in her hand at all times. I do, however, have the hope that my story will give others the courage to speak the truth of their lives and to be free.

The catalyst to Peace and Joy is humiliation.

Who established these rules?

Voice your pain in boldness; others reading your story can see that they too have a God-ordained purpose.

March 28, 2005: It is eight-thirty in the evening.

Comfort, listen to this, tonight I went to the movies and watched "Diary of a Mad Black Woman," written by Tyler Perry. I came away with a spring in my step. There were actually hopefuls still out there, men willing to allow the Holy Spirit of God to use their bodies as temples. Men with the P.P.R. qualities,...Protect, Provide, and Rescue their mates. On my drive home, I cried, I laughed,

I poured my heart out to God. I said to Him, "I am still alive. I am not crazy."

This enemy, Satan, tried to take everything, including my life. He confiscated my childhood memories, he raped my childhood innocence, and he took the faithfulness of my husband. He took my faithfulness from my husband. His attack on me broadened its stronghold in the societal abuse of my son falsely accused and denied an equitable opportunity for justice blinded by the evil of prejudice. Family and friends I trusted and trained in my business for many years turned their backs on me when I needed them most; hoping to destroy me even further. Extreme betrayals in human suffering.

Why not extreme betrayals? From the beginning of Creation, betrayals have marked the journeys of many chosen by God. Look at Joseph. His own brothers sold him into slavery because of their evilness, unaware that God allowed the evilness for the ultimate good.

> *"I am Joseph!" he said to his brothers. "Is my father still alive?" But his brothers were speechless! They were stunned to realize that Joseph was standing there in front of them. "Come over here," he said. So they came closer. And he said again, "I am Joseph, your brother whom you sold into Egypt. But don't be angry with yourselves that you did this to me, for God did it. He sent me here ahead of you to preserve your lives. These two years of famine will grow to seven, during which there will be neither plowing nor harvest. God has sent me here to keep you and your families alive so that you will become a great nation. Yes, it was God who sent me here, not you! And he has made me a counselor to Pharaoh-manager of his entire household and ruler over all Egypt.*
>
> (Genesis 45:3-8 NLT)

Through all of this, I am not dead. I am not dead. I am now even more alive because I did not die.

I am not crazy; I may-be a bit psychotic, but who isn't ?

I am still here.

The next two months will be spent in solitude with Mother/Father Divine. The command is for me to wade through the dung of a sordid past and extract the good.

Now that I have crossed over from living in denial, I need clarity, I need wisdom, I need understanding, and most importantly I need my blue print to purpose.

Marie Pinto, African American, Spiritual psychotherapist, don't forget Holy Ghost filled, is the soul chosen by God to walk with a sister down this most difficult path. As I observed Marie, and I call her Sister-friend-therapist, I am thinking, this wonderful soul of God has no idea our Father is about to use her to accompany me on a journey, a journey that will change her views and total understanding of who God is. She will meet our Father now as a lion, who will destroy for his children, and not as a lamb. I can hardly wait to get to the end of this season, because like you the reader, there, the long-awaited revelation of God's divine plan for my life will manifest itself. I know the purpose, a baton remember, but not the sojourner's path to lead me beyond my past solidly into His purpose for healing and reward. What I am confident about is that I am indeed His daughter divine, with the devil's garbage under my feet.

Comfort, You are so quiet. Perhaps that's a good thing, because I really need to get this stuff off of my chest. You really live by example. Remember, You told me You will not speak unless I am quiet.

Thank You for following Your own principle; I know it cannot be easy to listen to a story You already know.

"Be anxious for nothing...Why are you rushing this season?...Be anxious for nothing."

Thank You Father.

CHAPTER THREE

A Good Place...I Am in a Good Place

<u>March 29, 2005</u> 10:00 in the morning.

I met with Marie today. She reminded me I was in a good place. I shared with her what the Holy Spirit confirmed to me when He said, "Fear not, for thou shalt not be ashamed; neither be thou confounded, for thou shalt not be put to shame: for thou shalt forget the shame of thy youth, and shalt not remember the reproach of thy widowhood any more."

> Thank You, Father, because what I already remember, and what I believe is there to be revealed, and You say I won't be ashamed. Hey use me, I am Your daughter divine.

I also shared with Marie that after 22 years of marriage, I admitted to myself only last night, that I was indeed living a life of fantasy. I did not have a wonderful relationship with my husband. I lived in a fantasy world I invented for myself. There was no love, no honesty, and no respect. We both lost trust for each other 14 years ago when his child birthed by another woman entered the picture.

His betrayal was a deep gnashing wound, familiar and yet unknown. Why does this betrayal sit like a raging beast in my stomach? He seems so at home. Betrayal, that is. Why can't I rid myself of this damned beast? He knows me more than I know myself.

Marie seems to think and said so, "You no longer live in denial." Never knew I was. She said I had crossed over. Crossed over to what? She then started to act like she was the spirit of Elijah, looking for a root. Here we go again. I thought once Elijah found the root I am straight, ready, set, but nooooo. Miss Elijah claims the root has to be dug up. She said every one of us carry with us sometimes a special object that represents a special and sacred time in our lives. As she was speaking I started to sweat and tremble.

I told her about a little girl's dress that I have kept with me all these years. Whenever I would come across this dress in my closet it would always give me such comfort. Of course I did not recognize the feeling back then. The dress would fit a one or two-year-old child. Seafoam green is my most favorite color, I would paint just about every room I occupied this color.

While telling Marie about the dress and how I loved the color, my body temperature joined the sweating and trembling I was already experiencing. The color of the dress is seafoam green. How come I never recognized that? Okay, okay, where is this going? A mental break seems inevitable and in order.

<u>March 31, 2005</u>

How did Marie and I come to discuss my husband's child? I think today Marie has a screw loose somewhere; she is saying this child is crucial to my deliverance. She was planned by God and has value and purpose. (Did God really plan the adulterous acts of my husband? Is this not a contradiction?) Yet, I can agree, God plans us all with value and purpose.

What is she talking about? With a sense of foreboding, I am listening to Marie rattle on and on, how all children are planned and have a purpose. Right about now I am thinking, enlighten me, Elijah wife. Your husband's action brought me to the root of my inner conflict and now you dig it up. Explain to me, Father, how can Georgette be planned by You? At this point I am totally tuning out Marie. I know this woman is mad. This hurts.

Who is the psycho today? Finally Marie gets the hint, and asks for my attention. And girl friend just continues to speak as if there was no distraction; as I was saying, "Satan is the one to tempt us, but God uses our weakness, the opportunity we give Him with screw-ups." No way did God plan this adulterous act, but He is using this and now I must stand still to know His plan and have His peace.

That's why He says in His Word, all things work together for good to them that love God.

This young innocent girl and I are both victims of the sin of my husband, her father. Did You hear me Comfort? She even quoted scriptures. What is my Father's world coming to? Somebody please beam Marie back to earth.

"Antoinette, yes she is right."

"Suffer the little children to come unto Me and forbid them not, for of such is the kingdom of heaven."

You know what, this is getting a bit deep for me. Anybody here remember the principle of creeping before you walk?

"Why creep now, Antoinette?"

"You were so anxious to get this over with."

I am reminded here of a dream I had on October 2003. It was more like a picnic setting. I was standing in a lake and the water reached me just below my knees. There were kids swimming in the area where I stood. Suddenly, they all began to drown at the same time. I tried to save the child closest to me, but he kept slipping threw my fingers. I reached out my hand and saved the other children, but was unable to save the child closest to me. Where I stood the water was very shallow, but every time I reached in to pull out a child, the water became very dark and deep. The parent of the child that died kept trying to hurt me; she said I could have saved her child.

It is so weird how the Holy Spirit reminds us of dreams, visions, and conversations we have had in the past that certainly did not make sense at the time.

So, Comfort, what's up?

Please don't tell me Mother Divine is birthing a ministry out of my wound? Am I to comfort the children? I don't think so, and besides, she is only one child. You said comfort the children. Please don't tell me my husband has other children out there. These are some rather new developments, I never signed up for all this. Anyway we might as well finish the conversation.

Where are the other children?

"Antoinette, they are locked away within the souls of my daughters roaming the earth. Every time you look at a woman, a daughter of mine is in prison within her."

Are you trying to tell me that when You look at us, You see the results of abuse, rape, molestation, and abandonment? We are so hidden by sin, shame and fear, yet You know every one of us?

"Yes, Antoinette, my daughters are dying."

"It is time for them to come home."

"They were not created to live like this."

How will You get them home?

"Well, my plan was..."

Oh Lord! This is like a call from hell.

"That's right, I placed enmity between Satan and the Woman.

He wants all My daughters dead and lost. To curse Me and then die in their sins. I want my daughters home and alive. I am preparing a kingdom for them.

Suffer my daughters to come unto Me and forbid them not, for of such is the kingdom of heaven. Georgette represents all the daughters that come into this world unloved, undesired, displaced, and

seemingly without value. Georgette is you. You (too) are a married man's daughter."

I am?

Oh what a revelation, a painful revelation: No one ever told me my father was married.

What about Georgette's mother? What part of hell does she represent?

"Antoinette, please stay focused."

Okay, so Georgette has a purpose, an awesome purpose. What now?

"Is that a yes, Antoinette?"

"Will you allow Me to use you?"

Do I have a choice?

"Would you like Me to start the process all over again?

"That should give you enough time to make your decision."

Putting it that way, You sure have my attention. Let's see, if You had to do this all over again, I would be 82 years old. Do You mean I would still have to make this decision?

"Your purpose never changes."

"Age is not a condition or exception."

Father, You have my unconditional surrender. But remember, I have your ah…I-shall-not-be-brought-to-shame promise.

"Is that a yes?"

Yes, Lord, but just so we are on the same page, I would like to go over this promise with You. I would hate to have a misunderstanding later. Here goes, as You said in Your Word to me, "Fear not, for thou shalt not be ashamed; neither be thou confounded; for thou shalt not be put to shame: for thou shalt forget the shame of thy youth, and shalt not remember the reproach of thy widowhood any more."

"Antoinette, please rest."

Comfort, not that I always have to have the last word. But as You know there is a thin line, a really thin line between sanity and insanity. Would You say, I am, Ah… sane?

"Antoinette, please rest."

You want to use me and I take that as a yes. I am sane.

"A daughter that is in honor, and understandeth not, is like the beasts that perish. Now rest."

Chapter Four

Healing

May I be at peace,

May my heart remain open,

May I awaken to the light

of my own true nature.

May I be healed,

May I be a source of healing

for all beings.

adopted

Shattered Dreams

Each time it seems I make progress,
Disaster or problems arise
which puts my faith to the test
And attempts to vanish my smiles.
But I look to the Lord and ask, why?
Didn't I do my best?
In my mind I hear the reply,
Faith becomes stronger, when put to the test.

Then I start over again
To make true my shattered dreams.
Now doubt sets into my heart,
But I know its Satan's scheme
to shatter my dreams apart.

Now when I start afresh
For my shattered dreams to come true,
My mind is at rest
Because my trust is in God
For God leads the way for me to choose.

Betty Addison, October 17, 1995

For all that has been – thanks
For all that shall be – yes

I feel rested, truly at rest, Comfort, but so; so sore. How about if we get going? Yes, let's proceed. I know You said not to be anxious, that I should take this season slowly. But, I am so excited. Just thinking about Georgette, the pain escapes me; just a little sore is what I feel. I know You said, "Be not anxious" and that I should take this season of waiting, this time to know true patience, slowly.

I see her as Your daughter, therefore a sister/daughter to me. She no longer represents a threat, an intruder, an unwanted area of my life, a dirty secret. I accept, believe and embrace in my heart that she is a sister, a daughter to be saved.

How amazing the instant release from pain at the moment a decision is made. My decision is made. I will love my sister. I choose to release the years of pain, hate and anger that have held me a prisoner. I choose to be free.

So, Comfort, what now?

"Antoinette, take it slowly."

"Your spirit and soul has made the decision to love, we still have to deal with the flesh."

I hear You, Comfort, I know You said, "Be not anxious" and that I should take this season of waiting, this time to know true patience, slowly. How do I surrender completely to Your voice? Why is this instruction so difficult for me?

But, You mean its not over? When I see Georgette, a bucket of love will not just rush right out of me for her? Like I am her mommy?

"No Antoinette, every decision made in life has to go through a process. You have to be taught how to love yourself, before you will know how to love her. You have taken the most difficult step, you have made the decision."

Oh boy, why do we always seem to circle back to the Elijah business? I am about ready to lose his address.

"The spirit of Elijah will always be with you. He has a permanent position of keeping you holy and repentant before me. I hate sin, Antoinette, just as fiercely as I love you. Relax, your life is about to change in more ways than you can imagine."

"You will reap the fruits of your labor."

"You, my beautiful Antoinette are on your way home."

"You will show the way to many daughters."

"They will find the way home because of you."

"They shall come in all forms, conditions, colors, and backgrounds."

"Embrace them, show them my love, and show them the way home to me."

"They are my daughters, young and old, they are my jewels."

"I will anoint your heart, Antoinette, with a special gift of love so that you can and will embrace my daughters as they come into your life. My daughters have been through so much pain and anguish; they have cried so many tears. Their souls have cried out to me from the prisons of hell. They have watched their own daughters raped and molested. They have watched their sons imprisoned unjustly. They have been forced to prostitute their bodies for survival. They have laid their babies in the grave because of hunger."

"They have endured their husbands having other women, but did not have the strength to leave. Others have been given credit for sacrifices they have made with blood. Many have died because the heart could not take the anguish any more. They are like a fetus in the womb of a woman. They must be nurtured, loved, and protected."

"Do for them what I did for you."

Okay, Comfort.

April 2, 2005, and it is twelve minutes past two in the afternoon.

Comfort, I gave my husband a copy of section 1 of the manuscript.

I did not discuss with him what has been revealed to me or what I have been going through. I just handed him a copy.

Oh boy, what have I done?

Was this the correct way to do it?

I am sweating bullets here, and this man tells me he is really hungry, he would like to eat first. Well maybe that's a good thing. I will just lie here on the floor, and pray for a hole to open up. I am waiting on him, two minutes sure feels like two days. Maybe I should have spoken to Marie first. Well, too late.

Oh God, I really wish I had spoken to Marie first.

Maybe my husband needed to be prepared first. What have I done? Why is Flexi our cat so happy? Does he know what is going on here? I wish he would just sit at one place, so I can think. No, not think, sweat: I'm sweating.

Oh boy, my life story is on paper and this man is plating food. Suppose he holds on to the manuscript, my life story, for a few days, before he says anything to me?

Oh, Lord.

"Antoinette, stop. I am in control here."

You can say anything, Comfort; I do not see You sweating. What am I saying? Please Father Divine, Mother Divine, still the fast pace of my beating heart. I am a baby, and this is grown-up stuff.

"You know what I love about you, Antoinette? You are very honest about your feelings with Me. So many of My children pretend when they come before Me. They forget I see them every moment of every day. They forget I know their every thought. I am so disgusted."

"I love a daughter who can be honest before Me."

We worship Him in truth and spirit…oh to know You love me still, with all my ranting. Oh yes, like that time I wanted to curse. I was so angry about what was done to me as a child. You allowed me to curse without calling Your Name in vain. Thank You so much, that was really a load off my back. We sure got rid of that cursing demon. He came right out, rolled right off my tongue.

"I will ignore that. I shall bring healing to your body, soul, and spirit."

Oh yes, let me know when You are dealing with the healing of the body. I have some stubborn blackheads that just would not acknowledge the laying on of hands. And, You know I have had two children, so my stomach and my breast…

"Antoinette, what will it take for you to be quiet?"

Just say the word, and my mouth is outta here.

"Shut up. Is something wrong with your eyes? They seem to have gotten larger? That's my girl, relax."

I am thinking, whatever…

Comfort, can I sing?

My Jesus, I love thee

I know thou art mine,

For thee all the follies of sin I resign

My gracious redeemer

My Savior art thou

If ever I love thee

My Jesus it's now.

Oh Comfort, how I love that song. How I love You. I want to run, I want to jump, and I really don't know what to do. I am so happy. There is a warm feeling in my stomach. My hands are so warm, my back is feverishly hot. What's going on?

"It is called joy, Antoinette. You now know you are home, and you are beginning to feel happy."

Oh to experience true happiness. Yes, but I am still waiting on my husband to read the manuscript. Remember the horrid revelations of my childhood … he is about to come face-to-face with quite a different image of me, his precious, darling wife.

"Antoinette, remember my promise they shall surely gather together but not by Me. Any one that should gather together against you shall perish for your sake. You are covered my dear. You are My leading lady."

Okay, Comfort, I thank You. It really does not matter what my husband does. I no longer fear the demons of rejection, abandonment, and insecurity (I think).

"My daughter, be assured that you are indeed a force for God that will shake Heaven and Hell. Revelation is not for gratification but for obedience. Associate with anointed people, they will influence you, and that will produce marvelous effects. Guard the anointing carefully. And remember; it is I who have called you."

Thank You for choosing me, and still I pray protect me, Comfort, from deception and disobedience. Lead me not into temptation to return to the darkness that once bound me that it should never cloud my Spiritual eyes. The Holy Spirit and I fought every demon that came against me, and we were the victors. The devil had the nerve to even join me in a fast. At least he tried. (Go figure.)

In yet another dream, I was in a room surrounded by demons. The entire room occupied by the distinguishable presence of evil. Bodies masked the floor, the walls, the ceiling, and the windows. As I stood there wondering what to do, I saw an angel descending from heaven, untouched and seemingly unafraid of the demons. He came to protect me. I saw him leave heaven. He joined me in the room, and a door simply opened up. We left together.

There was another time I was sick for a whole week, and had not spent the necessary quality time with my friend, the Holy Spirit, in prayer. On my way home from work that Monday, in the quietness of the drive, I just said, "You know I really miss You." Immediately the power of Comfort's love suspended the car and carried me. My friend missed me also, and lifted me as one would a child. I had nothing to fear as His presence caused me to surrender my every motion to him. I did not even have to steer the car. I love You Holy Spirit! You are my friend.

Back in February 2004, I had a revelation of God's plan for my life, but of course I did not understand then. Oh Jesus, my husband is reading the manuscript. He keeps clearing his throat. Why does he keep coughing? Which page is he reading now?

"Antoinette, focus."

Okay, Comfort, "Fear not, for You are with me."

So, in this dream there were two groups of people holding hands. We were all lying on the ground waiting for the Holy Spirit to descend upon us. I could see the Holy Spirit making His descent. In my feeble attempt to peek and close my eyes at the same time; The Holy Spirit spoke within me, "Antoinette, you are waiting for Me to descend on you, and I am already within you. Your eyes must be opened always to watch My children. I have called you as a caretaker of My daughters." Back then, not knowing what the Holy Spirit was up to, I replied, "I accept Your assignment as a spiritual mother."

Why am I suddenly remembering all these things, Comfort?

"Antoinette, you are being healed. Your purpose and destiny is being revealed to you. Your healing has always been within your purpose."

Remember this dream Comfort? I was at a circus and bolts of fire were being thrown at a group of us. Even though I could not find a place to hide, for some reason the fire could not harm me. It was destroying everything around me, though. I eventually found myself at my mother's house waiting for my sister, Carolie.

"It's okay, Antoinette. Allow the memories to come. You are safe now. I have not lost one that my Father has given Me."

I used to always wonder why, whenever my husband would leave me to visit his relatives, such a dreadful feeling of abandonment and rejection would engulf me. How does a chosen child of God, experience such pain on a consistent basis? I know I did not hate his relatives, so what was this? Back in January 2005, I cried out to God for deliverance; from what, I was not too clear on except everything hurt. My frustrated husband dangling our fragile marriage before me with accusations of me constantly hating his relatives. His perception was that I hated his relatives, and I'll never be happy until I lose the hate. He said my hatred is so deep that I myself had no control. Are his perceptions valid?

An ever-present, deep dark loathing for the rejection and abandonment I endured as a child reawakened because my in-laws disrespected me and ultimately discarded me stirred the anguish from yesteryears. My husband offered me, his wife, no protection from their jeers and cruel treatment. More tears for the loneliness and dread I endured during my childhood and in my adulthood: DeJaVu. Circular pain as an adult...so many God-awful reminders of my mother's mental illness affecting my life. Mommy, she would suddenly become very sick: Manic-depressive. With no warning, the extreme episodes of manic behavior or her deep depressions would take a front and center seat in my frightening world. For a child who did not understand the signs of an acute episode…the oncoming illness always shocked me no matter how frequently it appeared.

In a rare family moment as we sat around feeling happy and safe, she would without any provocation or warning become manic. Her time spent in mental hospitals left me feeling abandoned. Now, the Holy Spirit reveals to me the pain I experience whenever my husband suddenly leaves, even though it was just for an away visit, the pain of the abandonment I felt as a child when my mother was suddenly taken away, is a familiar pain. Children were discouraged from visiting at the Mental Institute, so I could not accompany nor visit my mother. I am not welcomed at my in-laws' homes, and could not visit them with my husband.

Mommy's mental illness prevented her from protecting me as a young child. Is my husband mentally ill also?

As a child and an adult, my efforts to build protective walls against the people whom I thought hated and abused me seemed futile. The abuse always seemed to have a right to enter, and to force itself upon me. I could never quite protect myself against it. It just always seemed to have a right, as if I was the one in the way.

The Mental Institute was not physically doing anything to me, but I was not welcome; there was only room for my mother. My husband's relatives are not doing anything to me; I am just not welcomed in their lives.

I am so glad to know that after all these years I never hated them, rather I lived in fear of them because of what they represented to me.

Thank You, thank You, and thank You. God forbid that I should hate any of His children. Now I can really go on with my life. This taste of freedom really feels good.

Don't ask how I used to buy friendships. I would go to the extreme for others to the point of hurting myself financially because of my fear of abandonment.

I remember one day asking the Holy Spirit, "What is the plank in my eye?" He replied, "**Rejection, Abandonment, and Insecurity**."

My sisters and brothers, the way to honor God is to identify those familiar spirits that entrap us in unforgiveness and fear, and we all have them. Then we ask God for deliverance. Trust me, He is eager to deliver.

CHAPTER FIVE

The Spirit of Elijah Must Clear the Way

It is still April 2, 2005

I was on a phone call with my sisters Gillian Richards, who resides in Texas, and Minister Lillette George, a pastor in St. Thomas, Virgin Islands. Lillette is also the director of Hekima Women's Rescue Shelter, a ministry in mother's womb, on the way to the center of her heart. During the conversation, Lillette made a statement that I have used many times, but today had a reflective impact on my heart. She said, "In order for the Holy Ghost to come into our hearts in its full power, the spirit of Elijah must clear the way."

I am thinking, Elijah spirit, I am so sorry for griping about You. I guess the dirt doesn't have an easy time when it requires being razed, dug up, tossed around, and leveled for a new home: And still it rains on me. Perhaps, the inner workings of my heart shall appear beautiful as with a brand new house, and the constant rain will produce a beautifully manicured lawn leading to these massive doors of a new beginning. Why am I fighting this? Again, I am so sorry. Thanks for preparing me to receive the promises of heaven that are mine.

Comfort, what is going on? It has been over an hour since I gave my husband the manuscript. He is still clearing his throat.

"Antoinette, be still and know that I am God. Remember our covenant, you shall not be brought to shame."

That's right. Teach me patience, great Comforter, though I am blatantly impatient right now. I think a shower is in order here, 48 hours is definitely my limit. I know it does not bother You, Comfort, but I must comply with the laws of nature.

Talk to You later.

It is still April 2, 2005 and it's fifty-two minutes after five in the evening …

Well, my husband left and did not say anything to me. I thought I had no expectations and yet I am really sad. I really don't want to cry. I don't have enough energy to cry. Oh boy, here I go.

"Antoinette, in righteousness shalt thou be established; thou shalt be far from oppression; for thou shalt not fear: and from terror; for it shall not come near thee."

It's not working, Comfort, I really need to cry. Okay, I am beginning to feel better. That was pretty close.

April 3, 2005 and it is thirty-seven minutes past four in the morning…

Will daylight ever come? Comfort, my husband still did not speak to me.

He went to bed. So, I figured maybe the floor is a safer place for me to sleep tonight. (Can't fall off the floor, now can I?) I was restless but kept hoping that he would want to speak with me, but he did not. This is so disappointing. I could not approach him because I did not know what to say to him. I am not as sad this morning as I was yesterday; really weak, though.

Oh, I just got it. I am being taught not to depend on anyone for affirmation but You, Comforter. My God, in this walk with mother divine, it's very unlikely many would understand (these rules). Well Comfort, I welcome You this morning. I welcome You in this most narrowest of daylights. You are so worthy. I honor You. I praise You. I can feel Your heart beat within me, and Your presence flowing through my soul. I have taken a deep breath and feel myself coming alive. I didn't know my feet could be so happy, but they just began swinging all over the floor, oops…my bed. I am really beginning to feel happy and alive.

My life is still so uncertain (to me), and yet You find a way to allow happiness to enter. I honor You today. This healing process is moving rather rapidly, or is it hunger I am feeling? I haven't eaten in over two days. No, I am not hungry, I just feel rather special.

12:15pm

Comfort, I am suddenly feeling so weak. What is going on? I have to make it up the stairs. My head is so heavy and hot. Am I fainting? Or have I passed out? Why am I still writing? Okay I have not fainted; my phone is ringing; my friend Blondell is calling . Okay, I am now starting to cry. Why am I crying? Never mind, You can tell me later. Right now, Father, please help me. I am not giving up, I just need You to help me. I don't want to be sick. I want to finish this assignment.

My body continues to feel faded, or is it my mind going through the passages. Oh, Lord! Somebody downstairs started playing country-western songs. Oh boy! Please, Comfort, tell them to turn it down. I can't listen to this right now. Something about a shotgun and put her in the ground. It's still playing.

"Antoinette, trust in the Lord with all thine heart, and lean not unto thine own understanding. In all thy ways acknowledge Him and He shall direct thy path. Let the peace of God that surpasses all understanding, fill your heart. Receive God's peace."

I need You so much, Comfort. Right now, comfort me. Show me how to enter Your peace. Show me how to hold it together.. Please dry my eyes. Juanita said You know how to dry my eyes. She said Your peace is available today, and You are my peace. Where are You Peace Divine? I can hear Kathy saying to close my eyes and call You. I am calling, but where are You? My eyes are closed but I can't find You. I can't believe this.

I was already in bed, and You sent me to get a shower. You used the warm water to wrap me in Your womb. I remember when I was growing up I would run the shower as hot as I could handle it, and hug my body. I had that same familiar feeling tonight; protected, loved, and covered. All these years You used the warm water to cuddle me. You are amazing. You continue to surprise me and yes, to my heart's content. I welcome You Peace Divine. You are awesome. Good night.

<u>April 5, 2005</u>, and it is 9:42 in the evening

It seems I regressed into old, all-too-familiar behavior last night; extreme sadness and brokenness pierced my heart. It felt like there was a needle digging me in my chest. I know that I did not want to die, but the pain was so unbearable. Then You did the water thing. You are really something. I love You so much.

"Antoinette, your wound is like a pimple. As you apply proactive or acne medication the pimple heals from the other layer. You find that each time you squeeze that pimple there is less and less pus to extract. It heals gradually from the outside in. Each time you feel like you have regressed, remember the Holy Ghost is purging your soul of the pain from your past. If you notice, the duration of each regression is shorter and shorter in time. Remember when it would take four or five weeks to overcome a regression? Now look at you, 15 maybe 20 minutes, and you are back on track. Looks like the pus is drying up to Me."

Thank You Comfort, for helping me to see this wound as a pimple. Each setback purges me of the impurities from within; the poisons scarring my face, to set me free of them indeed. Before long, the pimple will disappear as if it never took root. Oh great! Comfort, are there still a lot of impurities in my pimple?

"Daughter divine, you are getting there. Do you feel like a pimple squeeze right now?"

No!

"Sounds like a progression to Me."

You know, Comfort, I was just thinking, on our journey You send people into our lives to walk with us for part of the way. However, we inherently find something wrong with these people. If only they would just understand our needs, pay us a little more attention, call us more often. But You know as I am getting to the end of this journey my needs are changing. If this friend, husband, companion, whatever, were to become what I needed at the time, I would become less tolerant of them when reaching the end of my journey. Why so? My needs change. I would be wondering why they don't get a life!

"Yes, Antoinette, as my daughters travel on this path to Me, I send them hope along the way. Instead of thanking Me for what I am doing, My daughters want Me to correct or change some character flaw in hope. These people are just representatives of what I am preparing for them. So be encouraged because at the end of the journey hope will be there. Satan has a way of using My tools to destroy My daughters. What happens, when I send them a symbol of hope, they forget or might not realize that they are on a journey. Satan fools them into believing that I have sent them a Mr. Right. What seems like Mr. Right is only a symbol of the real thing. Do not be fooled, even my workmen at times forget their assignments and allow self to get in the way. Hope will be at the end of your journey, don't be fooled. At this stage in the game for life, the Bible principles are your only safeguard. When Satan begins to use the workmen I have sent, there is always a Bible principle being broken. In this realm you have a different anointing at work. My daughter, it feels right, but it is oh, so wrong. It is a trap of your enemy. Your flesh is a liar from the pit of hell. The Bible principles are your only safe guard.

Don't trust your feelings. Remove yourself and observe what I have sent you as a symbol of hope. In Satan's hand this symbol of

hope now becomes a symbol of hopelessness with no teeth, no job, a church with 3 members, strange looking hair, and don't forget pitiful looking. These symbols of hope no longer acknowledge Me as the Holy Spirit when working for Satan. Check them out, they always say, Oh Father said this, or Father said that. Take a good, good look. At this point you will also notice that this person cannot walk two blocks, they need a ride. You have suddenly become their chauffeur. Or, someone is trying to poison them, or they saw someone hiding behind a tree pointing a gun at them. Oh, they always can see angels around, but somehow the angels are not revealing themselves to you. Look out for this line, you both were sent here together from heaven, and you met at the crossroad, so God needs each anointing to accomplish His plan. Every time you meet, you must touch. That is a demon from the pit of hell, my daughters. Hope turned to hope-less. Do not walk away - run. Hope's job is done, he is now hope-less. The tool used is manipulation.

Pride can be the motive if we always want people to know when and how God speaks to us. At this stage in the game, hope-less wants to know everything that God says to you, so that you can compare notes, as if God starts a sentence with you and finishes it with him. Of course you are willing to share because at this point the fear that you have been wrong overwhelms you. The demon of pride now hands you over to the demon of denial. Stop, my daughters.

Do not call, do not accept any calls. Do not meet with this demon. Discard any gift you might have been given, it came from the dollar store anyway.

Go back to your secret place with God. Check with the Holy Spirit before you share, when you share, and how much you share. Don't worry about hope-less; trust Me, he will disappear. He cannot function after he has been discovered: Darkness is his cover.

This kind of wisdom is based in humility. When pride comes, then comes shame and denial; but with the humble is wisdom (Proverbs 11:2, NKJV).

Timing is important. Often, the greater revelation we receive from God, the more discernment is required about if or when we should share it. If you serve Me with this attitude, I will find pleasure in you. In looking into your past, you will hurt from the mistakes, but do not hate. Remember the pimple."

God, You are speaking so much into my heart. Teach me obedience.

"There is a book written by Iyanla Vanzant, *The Value in the Valley*. Read the book. My daughter was inspired. The time has come for My daughters to step out of the shadows of their lives and into the spotlight. It is time to be free from our failures that we might be free to succeed.

Discipline yourselves with this higher goal in mind. Run not with un-certainty but with certainty. I have chosen you as My vessel. Everything you need for the greatest performance of your life is already within you."

Yes, I understand. I remember Joyce Meyers listing 10 points for keeping my joy:

1. Stop trying to figure everything out.
2. Mind your own business.
3. Choose your battles.
4. Live one day at a time.
5. Pray about things early.
6. Be positive.
7. Live with a clean conscience (at this point after you repent).
8. Follow peace.
9. Talk positive.
10. Make others happy.

I hope I can remember them. Long list, Joyce.

Comfort, I remember one day the Holy Spirit brought such peace to my soul. Fear caused me to say some really bad things in the past.

I always felt as if I was letting down the Holy Spirit with so much doubt and confusion in my life. I was a bit afraid that Feminine Divine did not know how much I loved her. As I thought this over, the Holy Spirit spoke into my spirit and said, "I have forgiven you for the bad things you have said in the past. God has not changed His plans concerning you. Most of what you said and did came through fear."

I am not the easiest person to teach; You might have figured that out by now, and yet Mother Divine never gave up on me.

"Antoinette, it is the Lord who goes before you.

"He will march with you, He cannot fail you nor let you go nor forsake you. Let there be no cowardice, or flinching, rather fear not, neither become broken in spirit (depressed, dismayed, and unnerved with alarm)."

Comfort, the Holy Spirit ministered to me so powerfully today from *The Elijah Task*, written by John and Paula Sanford. He said, "There is a change, a deep and abiding change, that is taking place deep within your well and a new flowing of the rivers of My life shall arise within you. For you will touch more and more the throne of My grace and from within shall waters proceed unto many broken-hearted and wounded spirits with renewing and rejuvenating power. For you have found a key and I shall unlock the doors of opportunity for you in the near future to embark upon the great sea of adventure. For you shall be released of your present situation in a way that will both startle and delight you, and you shall be free in Me to do My bidding. Wonder not how the Lord shall perform His Word. I say not how, neither are you to wonder how. But in a most startling way you shall be free."

I trust You, Comfort. Thank You. And one more thing, I have slept on the floor for two nights now. My back is hurting, so safe or not, I am sleeping in my bed tonight.

"That's My daughter. Antoinette, remember this always. Those who are reflecting the light of God will cherish a loving disposition.

They will be cheerful, willing, and obedient to all the requirements of God. If you yield to the claims of God and become permeated with His love and filled with His fullness, children, youth and young disciples, will look to you for their impressions of what constitutes practical godliness; and you may thus be the means of leading them in the path of obedience to God. You will thus exert an influence which will bear the test of God, and your work will be compared to gold, silver, and precious stones, for it will be of an imperishable nature."

Chapter Six

A Bubbling in My Heart

Comfort, at this precise moment there is a bubbling in my heart I can hardly describe.

Back in January of 2004 I attended the first Institute of Mentoring directed by Judy Jacobs. Shirley Arnold, Karen Wheaton, Prophetess Veter Nichols, and many others ministered to a group of over 250 women that weekend. That was a weekend I will never forget for the rest of this life, and into eternity. I am limited as to the words necessary to describe the awesome presence of God that I experienced. The experiences were of such a nature that they had to be kept in my heart. I thank you for my sisters, and their willingness to be obedient to the call of God on their lives.

Sisters, if we don't meet each other here again, I will see you in the Kingdom.

I'll be there.

"These women were your mentors. It's not about a crowd that can glorify the name of Antoinette, it is about the one that will glorify the name of God in her community, and by her life win that community. The name of Jesus must be praised: At His name every knee shall bow and every tongue confess that Jesus Christ is Lord."

Now I understand what Mother Divine meant when I was told that this is the ministry of Jesus, and that I must be obedient, I must wait upon Him always.

Comfort, I have not always been obedient. I really did not understand.

"I know, Antoinette. But now that you do understand, will you become obedient?"

But what about the other things that may happen that I might not understand? Can I assess the situation and make my own assumptions? I have made some pretty good ones in the past.

"Antoinette, total obedience is my condition. Will you be obedient?"

Give me a minute. Obedient. With my mind, I am thinking, and You want me to yield to You, Comfort, Your every command, without question? With an analytical mind, for I am a thinking woman...but Your thoughts are above mine, and Your ways past finding out. You are calling me into obedience? You will teach me regardless of myself; my flesh; to know Your voice and obey?

The Holy Spirit has placed me in some not-so-nice situations before. Sometimes He tells me one thing, and tells others something different. Have me looking kind of foolish. But you know, everything worked out for my good. And I have only ended up in those situations when I have revealed something He did not release me to reveal. Now I see, obedience will give me spiritual ears, willing to listen for Your voice and move at Your command with that peace which passeth all understanding. Lord, help me remember this from now on, that all things work together for good to them who love God, and are called according to His purpose.

Comfort, I am ready to obey. I will be totally obedient to Your directions from now on. But, just suppose I am not sure it is You?

"Antoinette, you know My voice and I always send a witness. To be a trusted and privileged daughter of Jesus Christ requires total surrender. Surrendered people obey God's Word even when it doesn't make sense to them. Surrender is best demonstrated in obedience and trust. Surrender is not the best way to live; it is the only way to live. Nothing else works!"

Yes, You are right. I will obey.

"Now, my dear daughter, you shall enjoy the benefits of a purpose driven life. There will now come meaning to your life, purpose to your life, there will be focus. Your life will be motivated, and you will know that you are being prepared for eternity."

It is amazing the steps God takes to guide us to His order, our destiny. We have no excuse, for His plan is ultimately for our good and His glory. Some experience fewer hardships and did not make it. We are overcomers; survivors. The Father wants us to have the joy He has promised when we walk into the gifts He provides to complete our assignment; He is with us because He is for us.

"Antoinette, no longer should you complain about the rejection, abandonment, lies, or anger. The mistakes made, they were all necessary to move you to a higher level in the Lord. That's the greatest need of the Elijah Spirit, to expose evil directly or cause it to surface for the purpose of repentance.

"It's all right for God's servants to be humiliated and seemingly of little value before men. It serves God's purposes. The humiliation works God's glory deep within their hearts. Your father is not afraid to embarrass you before the world."

I am definitely seeing eye-to-eye with You on that one!

"But oh, the rewards, not just here in this life but in the life to come. It is God who has kept and protected you. He shall be with you in trouble; He shall deliver you and honor you. You need not fear the heights. He is worth it.

"He will always catch you; and set you upright one more time than you can fall. Spiritual growth is when you realize that you cannot take on this warfare alone. You need your sisters. If you believe that you can win this battle alone, you have already lost. No daughter of mine is an island by herself; you need each other to survive."

"Meet together, pray together, encourage each other, and trust each other. No one can steal or take your purpose from you; it is exclusively yours."

"So, My daughters, live a little, in fact, live a lot. David knew the will of God; he simply did not follow the way of God!"

Yes, teach me Your will, Abba Father, Daddy, show me Your way.

"Yes, your focus must be changed from a seeker's need to God's agenda. When you turn to hear the voice of God, the real challenge becomes, to come up higher: No more horizontal living, but an upward growth. God's perspective always brings in the new.

"God's desire is that you forget the past. He is doing a new thing."

"Judy, my daughter who sees the white horses coming, likes to say, press, push, and pursue."

You are the best comfort. Teach me how to help my other sisters.

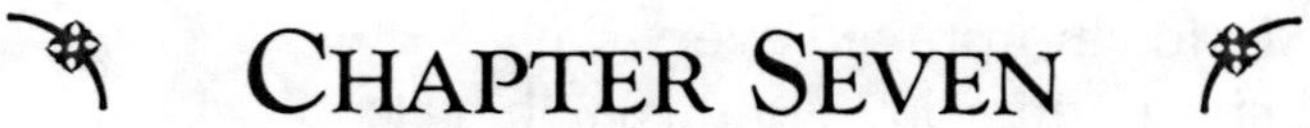

Chapter Seven

How Old is the Soul?

Forgetting those things that are behind, and reaching forth unto those things, which are before me. I press toward the mark for the prize of the high calling of God, Which is in Christ Jesus.

(Philippians 3:13-14)

Pick Up the Pieces

I feel broken, I feel spent.
My mind is burned out, and my heart has a huge dent.
No not a dent, more like a hole.
I've been kicked and stabbed so many times that I feel like a pole.
You known the ones for kung fu, and such,
They are always hitting and punching so so much.
They have no feelings and neither do I.
I was so numb from being hurt, I wondered why I wouldn't die.
Does God ever look down to this cold hard place?
I know if he did, he would see the pain on my face.

I was hurting so bad, I just wanted to give up,
Like Jesus back then, why give me this cup?
I know that I am special, or it wouldn't hurt like this,
If I ended up dead, would I ever be missed?
I tried to live right, and do what was good,
Even when I was knocked down it wasn't for good.
I kept on believing that there had to better,
It was out there some-where, and would come sooner, not later.

So hope I did, and prayed every day,
that in a short while, joy would say hey!
Then one day she did, with a very sweet smile,
And oh boy, when I saw her I just stared for a while.
Feeling so happy; that finally I could smile.
"What took you so long?" she said,
"I've been waiting a while."
You have, I thought, and what about me?
I've been in prison all my life, its name is misery.

But forget all that, because I'm glad that you are here.
I hope that you're a nurturer, 'cause I need lots of care.
My heart is wounded, but I think I will live,
If you just give me love, and I learn to forgive.
So please help me move on, and pick up the pieces,
With you in my life, the pain finally ceases.

Neil Gregson

April 6, 2005, and it is two o'clock in the afternoon.

I really don't like what I am feeling right about now. Let me attempt to explain: I feel like a person who has been told that the doctor has found cancer in their body. You have dealt with the pain of the cancer for many years. A few weeks before the scheduled date of the operation, you are advised that the doctor will indeed to perform the surgery, but you will not be sedated. Well, that's how I feel; like I am about to undergo surgery, but I will not be sedated. God is about to or has begun this procedure to save my soul, and He has not and will not use any anesthesia.

Living through this season of my journey is proving to be a bit difficult. Literally, my body aches and there is such pain that's all too new and yet familiar. No denying something is gripping me. I would really love to go to sleep as my flesh slowly succumbs to this overbearing sense of change coming my way. How do I describe that which I can barely comprehend?

Dare I ask for a glimpse of what is about to come? I know you have been there. Would you say you feel like you are been pushed into the operating room on a gurney, and you are fully aware of what's going on, but you don't have the strength, power or desire to change anything? I couldn't stop it anyway because it has got to happen, otherwise my spirit will give up the ghost.

Soon I will be done, wid the troubles of the world,
The troubles of the world.
The troubles of the world.
Soon, I will be done wid the troubles of the world,
Going home to live wid God.

I would totally agree.

Oh, I am still sleeping on the floor. I feel dirty. I'm Your daughter, lovingly created in Your image; so I know I'm not dirt. Somehow, though, I cannot seem to feel clean enough to go back into my bed. But it is still raining. Where is all the rain coming from?

You know what I would really like at the end of all this, Comfort? A safe place to take a hot shower, and the freedom to really cry: My soul is in need of a safe place to open up and cry. I need to cry. Do You have any suggestions, Comfort?

Here we go again, I really, really feel like cursing. Why? I mean, didn't we get rid of that cursing demon? Comfort, please answer.

April 7, 2005 and it is eighteen minutes past 8 o'clock in the morning.

Comfort, I cannot believe You have not answered me. Whose side are You on? Why am I being treated this way?

"Antoinette, I can hear you."

Well, answer. You place me on a gurney, wheel me into the operating room, open me up for surgery, and now You choose to be quiet.

Makes a daughter want to curse. Each time I think I understand You, You shift on me.

"Antoinette, listen to Me. You were traumatized at a very young age. Your physical body matured, but it still houses a damaged soul. Your body, soul and spirit have to be healed and brought to maturity. Your soul needs a sabbatical, an extended sabbatical. Your soul has been crying out for a very long time, and you did not recognize the tears of the soul."

Comfort, what does the crying of the soul sound like?

"Antoinette, remember the times you would cry and sound like a horse? You would cry and just had no control over the strange sounds you were making?"

You used to hear me, Comfort? You were there all the time?

"I was right there watching over you. I would sometimes send you one of my helpers to dry your crying eyes. You were always broken. I am glad your soul won't have to cry like that anymore. Your flesh will be doing the crying from now on."

Comfort, I know for the body You use a knife, for the spirit You use the sword of the Word. What do You use to heal the soul? Not that I don't trust You, but I have a major problem with surprises.

"Antoinette, be patient."

I have been patient since last night. I went directly to sleep. I didn't ask you any more questions; that is, after the last one.

"Antoinette, My child, please be patient."

Okay. Teach me patience, oh Lord. Please.

<u>April 7</u>, continued, 9:12am.

I am an hour early for my appointment with Marie, my psychotherapist. Do you remember her? While I sit here in my car I am wondering, what surprise does girlfriend have for me today? Should I just sit here or should I go in? Well, I think I'll just sit here for a while and enjoy the weather. I purchased this book, *The Transformation of the Inner Man*, written by John and Paula Sanford; I might as well start reading it right now. My inner man needs some transforming right about now. This book is kind of thick. Hope it's not an indication of how long I will be on the operating table.

LIKE DAVID I PRAY:

Save me, O God, by thy name, and judge me by thy strength.
Hear my prayer, O God: give ear to the words of my mouth.
For strangers are risen up against me,
and oppressors seek after my soul;
They have not set God before them.
Behold, God is mine helper;
the Lord is with them that uphold my soul.

Oh Father, right here I thank You for Wendy Nicholas, Ray Howard, Inez Picart, Blondell Henry, Sandy Brown, Marie Pinto, Kathy Spaar, Janice Guider, my stepfather Uncle Joe, my sons Kerry and Kemyoe, my sisters Gillian and Lillette, Pastor Joseph McKenzie and Mayor L. Harvey Smith of Jersey City. I bless them right now. These are the ones You have chosen to uplift my soul. I know others are out there I am not aware of and I thank You for them. I would not have had the strength, endurance, or courage to do this.

You shall reward evil unto mine enemies, cut them off in thy truth. I will freely sacrifice unto thee; I will praise thy name, O Lord, for it is good. For he hath delivered me out of all trouble; and mine eye hath seen his desire upon mine enemies.

(Psalm 54)

"Antoinette, how old is your soul?"

How old is my soul?

"Yes, how old is your soul?"

Funny question. I don't know, but I would guess if I am 41 years old, that's how old my soul would be. I came into this world with a soul, and I have been here 41 years.

"Antoinette, I need you to listen attentively. I have many daughters and sons who have been victimized, traumatized at a very young age. Their souls locked away in bodies that become the prisonhouse of the soul, as their bodies experienced the evil Satan pre-planned for them. Yes, Satan had a tailor-made plan for each child of mine entering this world. He wants to destroy you before you can accomplish the purpose I have sent you here for.

"The tool I use to heal the soul is the integration of the necessary reminders of the past, and the revelation of your purpose. Your soul needs this vacuum to evolve."

Comfort, You made a mistake, You said sons. You have special sons also?

Sons, called chosen and anointed? Sons sent here with a divine purpose?

"Yes, Antoinette, I have many sons, sons whose souls are also locked away in prison; and they long to be free. I love my sons as fiercely as I love my daughters. They are your brothers divine. Your brothers are also traveling on their journeys to a Mother's heart. They need your love, your support, your encouragement, and your commitment to see them through. You, my children, are so precious to Me. You are created in My image. Satan's hatred for you is how he reveals his hatred for Me. He hates you as powerfully as I love you, because I have chosen you. If you want to get him really mad and immobile, love one another. You all have different personalities, different character traits, but guess what? It's me. The trait you hate so much in each other is who I am. As My children, when you

are not fully surrendered and restored, you tend to hate even the harmless flaws in each other."

- "I am fat."
- "I am thin."
- "I am rich."
- "I am poor."
- "I am an introvert."
- "I am an extrovert."
- "I am God."
- "I am what you sometimes hate in one another, so love me instead."
- "Bless each other."
- "If you can't speak the good about each other, don't say any thing."
- "Satan uses your tongue to curse one another."
- "His evil could not survive if he could not use you as vessels; so bless each other, bless each other, and bless each other."
- "Come to one another's rescue."

I will Comfort.

CHAPTER EIGHT

I'm Listening to When Leaders Are Called

> *Above all, you must understand that no prophecy in Scripture ever came from the prophets themselves or because they wanted to prophesy. It was the Holy Spirit who moved the prophets to speak from God.*
>
> (2 Peter 1:20-21, NLT)

After a leader is called, prepared and sent, the way that the business administration of God's affairs is handled is most important to Him, and incidentally to those He is raising to go forward. A highly anointed ministry is vulnerable to shame without proper administration skills, and godly character.

There are many leaders called, prepared, and sent who did not wait on God for that special gift of integrity and humility. They sometimes even refuse to accept, but instead look down at the help God has sent to them. So instead of being the conduit for blessings as God intended, the ministry becomes the source Satan uses to confuse God's children and abort the process of lacking nothing when Jesus promises us a life of abundance.

The training of a leader is a most difficult and humiliating time in that person's life. It is not uncommon to experience a season of quietness while waiting to hear the voice of God. Only He can give you the Divine revelation of your assignment and He will do so using the Holy Spirit to guide you, shaping and molding you with the anointing needed, so that the godly character needed to perform His will, will be demonstrated and lived through you.

Without integrity, those who have grown up in a very poor, maybe even a poverty-stricken environment may find the temptation of receiving gifts surprisingly strange. Alternatively, those leaders born into a wealthy family may find themselves in an awkward situation as well, particularly as ministries immorally compete amongst each other. Such gain is not a curse as we walk in the divine plan God has devised. The chosen seal of God is upon you.

When trusted with a special gift of integrity and humility, not just the measure of, rather, the gift of success that comes with walking into our purpose can destroy us. Like Paul instructs, we must always remain humble, reachable and most important, teachable, so that after we have shown others the way to the kingdom, we ourselves will not lose our way.

Daily, practice some task as a reminder that humility is most important. Pride and lack of humility are the greatest downfall of many anointed leaders. Always seek God and this will lessen the flesh's need to criticize or judge others. In the singleness of our human body, the physical anatomy consists of many body parts and they are all interdependent for the best possible outcome. When body parts or functions begin to turn against each other, science labels this as some form of autoimmune disease or deficiency.

The same is true with the Body of Christ: We might want to believe that the finger is not as important as the eye. The Body is not completely whole if a part of it is missing; the Body in fact becomes weakened or diseased when it turns on itself. God is a God of beauty and completion. Every member of His Body is not only needed, but has great value, and becomes absolutely necessary for the fulfillment of His promises.

Again, neither daughter nor son standing as an island or alone can complete the body of Christ. When you isolate yourself, you choose to weaken the entire Body, and, most importantly, the Body needs you for wholeness. We are sometimes fooled into believing this "religion" or that "order" completes the Body of Christ, but in God's eyes we might just represent the fingernail of His plan. Isolation is one of the great weapons of Satan.

God so wants us to passionately walk into the gifts entrusted to us; yet, we must be careful to not allow the rewards of our obedience to sideline our true purpose. To the glory of God, we lead, as He has called us. To the glory of God, we obey. To the glory of God we accept His rewards for obedience and seek to remain humbled by His love.

Chapter Nine

In God's Spirit

April 8, 2005 and it's 10 minutes after 11 o'clock…late morning.

Comfort, I feel really good in my spirit today. The squeaking of the gurney's wheels is not as irritating as before. Even the breath of the compassionate attendant is not so weird after all. I choose to always bless the earth. Always speak good, and not evil.

Father Divine depends on us.

He wants His prodigal children peacefully home. That includes you and me. There is an inheritance waiting that only our Father Divine will reveal. The blessings you will realize here on this earth because of your obedience, is but a shadow of the rewards to come. Eyes have not seen, nor ears heard, neither has it entered the heart of man, the things and plans God has prepared for His children.

Recall the faith and obedience of Abraham, Isaac, and Jacob, and God fulfilling His promises made to them: Those promises are yours and mine. Embrace, embrace, and embrace them! They were all tested through the most difficult of trials and yet gave obedience to God's call; because of the faith and obedience to God's call on their lives, a future and hope belong to all who are called. You are special, favored, called, and anointed. Your earthly rewards and promises are within your God-ordained purpose.

The sacrifices we are called to make, the humiliation we must endure is so small, when compared to the price Jesus Christ, the Son of God, had to pay. None of us are called to pay the price of humiliation and shame such as He did. There are things Jesus endured that were not written nor recorded, but trust only Jesus could redeem us from our sins, and He has done just that! Whatever is happening in your life, remember there is nothing new under the sun: If it happened to you, it happened to Him. Yet He arose and lives now.

Being raised from the dead, He now sits at his Father's right hand, interceding on our behalf. You will live after you have taken up your cross.

April 8, 2005, and it's now one-thirty in the afternoon.

Comfort, my friend Blondell just called; she started singing the song, "*I just called to say I love you.*" Now, Comfort, You have often endured Blondell's singing. But You know I said to her; "Keep on singing, your voice is bringing a melody into my soul. (And it was, I just did not say what type of melody.) Sister kept right on singing.

"Antoinette, I am so happy I created you. You amaze me. Where do you find the strength to joke in the mist of your pain?"

I guess because I now know where I am going.

I know my life is about to change.

I know my past and present circumstances, do not dictate my future.

I now fully understand the purpose of the cross.

I understand and accept the freedom it represents to me.

The cross is not just the wood that Jesus was nailed on; the cross is His arms open to save me.

"Antoinette, listen and share this with My children. Satan knows those I have chosen and sent into this world. You, My children, are all batons in My hand to bring about restoration. Satan, knowing this, uses the time of preparation I allow, to use My restorers as he chooses, but only as I allow. That is why those whom I have called and chosen, have all endured such suffering, rejection, humiliation

and anguish. His charge against you is that you will never make it back home after he is done with you, and has totally ruined you as a vessel that could be used by God. This he plans because he knows the hatred Father Divine has for sin. But Jesus is your vindicator. He reminds Father Divine of His blood, it fills in all the cracks in the vessel. It works every time."

"As My restorers pick up their crosses and follow Jesus into a life of surrender, that's another baton that has been raised out of hell. Antoinette, I can hear the melody of My choir singing in unison as I raise My batons. The choir members will never come to full attention unless the Choir Master and leader Jesus has His chosen batons surrendered and under His control. The chosen baton must, however, be willing, and make that choice to be used as a vessel. Before the baton is so called, to many it appears as a useless piece of wood, mud, and maybe even has unsightly fungus growing all over it, and incidentally that's the only time Satan wants or can use this seemingly valueless piece of stick.

"Oh, but look at that piece of wood after it is rescued, cleaned, shaped, polished, and sent for its purpose. The filth it was is no longer visible. Its past is no longer important to the Choir Leader. At this point one would get into grave trouble with the Choir Leader if that baton is condemned or reminded that it is just a piece of stick. It is now the Choir Master's baton. For the rest of that stick's life and into eternity, it is known only as a baton."

"Maybe an active baton, maybe an inactive baton, a valuable baton, nevertheless."

I really thank You, Comfort, for sharing with me all that You have, You are indeed the best, and I love You very much. Thanks for waiting for me at the end of my journey, even though it took me so long to get here. Without the difficulties of this journey, I would not know now who I really am. It is so necessary to know who Satan is and all that he is capable of, to understand and know who we really are. To know how much You need us. Thanks for dealing with my questions and most of all my hardheadedness. Satan made sure I knew his character. I am so happy You allowed me to know Yours. You are all right in my book. I love the fact that You are so down to earth. You are not up tight.

You are humorous. You tell me when I get on your nerves. I didn't know You had nerves. You even told me to shut up once, remember? You allowed me to speak when You sometimes needed me to listen. You cuddled me when it was necessary. You whipped my behind when it was needed (I got lots of those). You allowed me to curse when it was necessary for my healing (not calling Your Name in vain).

Can I tell You some of the words I can say without calling Your Name in vain?

"Antoinette, please, I will continue this conversation later. Bye for now. What am I going to do with that child? She really talks too much. Why did I ever choose her to be a voice on earth?"

I heard that, Holy Spirit, remember, You are now inside of me.

"What have I done? I can have no secrets from this daughter of Mine.

"She should probably be given a spiritual sleeping pill. Right about now she needs to sleep."

I would not take it. Remember, not that You can't, but You won't force me to do anything. I have choices. I oh I, yes, yes, yes, I can make choices, I won't, I won't, I won't take any spiritual sleeping pill.

Comfort, can I show You the dance I made up?

"Go ahead, Antoinette."

I won't, I won't, won't take any spiritual sleeping pill (jump)
I won't, I won't, won't take any spiritual sleeping pill (spin)
I won't, I won't, won't take any spiritual sleeping pill (leap)

Oh boy, I am out of breath.

Comfort, are You still there?

"Yes, Antoinette, and I have a question for you."

What?

"How old is your soul?"

Oh! More like 2 years old?

"Exactly, now please behave."

Abba Father, how great it is to feel like daddy's little girl again without all that weight of condemnation. What is that in Your hand, Comfort? Why the glass of water? Dare I believe You are really going to shut me up?

"Finally. That child just will not be quiet with her eyes open."

Thank You, Father, that in your Sovereign will You have called me into quietness. Surely, my mind needs the rest to enter into Your perfectly planned season of transformation. I close my mouth now and open my heart to You. Amen.

Chapter Ten

Restoration

Weeping has endured for a night,
And now joy has indeed come.

From Darkness to Light

Blinded by darkness
Couldn't see my destiny
Or my dreams put into reality
Until Christ shed His light upon me.
Father, you brought me through!
By circumstances and people
Dreams, faith, hope and trust
And, of course, your angels too.

Praise God for channels
That made me anew
To conquer dark tunnels
I alone couldn't do.

The light is shining brighter now
For I know Christ's revealing hand
Faith is stronger
Have no doubt
I will be able to stand.

Written by Betty Addison

April 5, 2005, and it is 4 minutes past six o'clock in the evening.

Satan is a liar. Everything he ever said to you was a lie. Look into the mirror. Touch yourself, touch your skin, and look into your eyes. You are real and powerful, and have a divine purpose. Let your soul take pause to consider, we are all convicted that every unhealthy and ungodly thing that has been done to us and by us, was to convince our souls that we have no value, and we were not created in the image of God.

Now that you have listened in on my conversation with Comfort, let's begin the restoration process together.

"Antoinette, please, one more thing. Tell my daughters what I have told you. Affirm them this day."

Yes, Comfort, I will.

Daughters of Mother Divine, please listen. Comfort wants you to know that in every daughter she has planted a ministry. It is not your nerves telling you that you can start that business or that you can go back to school to be a nurse (yes at 44), and 0 college credits. Nothing is too hard for you with God! You can supervise that factory, you can start that women's shelter, and you can pilot that aircraft. Created in the image of God, every daughter is born a victor, not a victim. What the world sees as failure or adversity, God uses to build His character within us that we may succeed in life and to have much success and all for His glory. Knitted in your genes by the love of God are the necessary ingredients for His divine plan. You are already equipped. Never is life the result of an accident or poor planning.

God needed the DNA of your father and mother to create the unique you. You are special and one of a kind. If you don't step into your purpose, it will be left undone throughout eternity. You might have come into this world as a result of your mother being raped, your father having an affair, or a teenage mother who gave you up for adoption. However the temptation was presented, your Holy Father used the opportunity to bring you into this world. All things really work together for good to them that love God. To them that are called according to his purpose. A good thing happened when you entered this world. You are indeed special, privileged, called, and chosen. You are here on a mission.

Every time you think that you cannot make it, just stop and look at the sisters who made it. We all had to go through the same preparation, because the goal is the same. Different circumstances, same goal, all for the character of Christ.

Have you not noticed that the Bible, written by men, inspired by God, waded through horrific storms and trials, and were then delivered with the plan of God for their success. The testing of their faith, like gold tried and re-tested rendered a trustworthy and prepared servant.

Anything or anyone entering your life who takes your joy, your peace, and diminishes your commitment to God is a demon from hell. Rebuke it. If you are not sure, rebuke and bind it anyway. The Holy Spirit understands and will accept your apology later. Remember, my dear friend, my forever companion, Spirit of Elijah, he will be right there to guide you to repentance.

Go ahead, step out in faith. Laugh a little; dance a little (in fact, a lot). As my friend Janice wrote to me and I share with you, (As I read this, Antoinette, I imagined the voice of God, Abba Father, full of laughter and extending this great foot…saying, "My daughter, plant your feet on Mine and dance with Me. **Let Me lead you, though**. Then He swung me around and instantly the freedom as I surrendered to His protective love, and protection enveloped me fully. He gave back to me the freedom to live again as a young girl, untouched, unscathed by the evilness of this world. He made me pretty and innocent, free. Together we danced and I stayed there forever in that safe, beautiful place."

Claim your freedom, even though there are still mistakes to make. Have faith to believe that even though the mistakes are inevitable He will provide the correct path for you. Your Father is not up-tight, religion is up-tight, and He is a God full of forgiveness and laughter.

Feed your soul with the righteous laughter of God on your journey and possess passionately the gift of His joy as it strengthens you. This is your right.

Create that new dance, that new laugh; I have one that I will share with you. Oh, not too much talking about what's happening. You see you won't get the stories straight until you get to the end of your journey. If you keep sharing every bit of revelation, you kind of start sounding like a liar. It takes sometimes as much as three or four years after you have been called and you have accepted or yielded to the call, for Mother Divine to prepare you. If you are called as a prophet or apostle your preparation can take up to fourteen years. You won't be prepared and sent any sooner if you talk less. You will certainly have less stress. Our Father has a timetable marked by His order and He is the keeper.

Sometimes self sounds like the Holy Spirit, so the less talking you do the better. Trust me when I say, keeping your mouth shut will produce less stress.

Mind your own business and focus on you during this preparation time. It is not a sin to say no. Allow people to make their own decisions, and be a supporter instead of an advisor. Do not waste time trying to convince anyone of your calling: Your calling is between you and the Great Shepherd who has chosen you.

To some listeners you may sound crazy, (this I know) especially if the DNA from mommy or daddy is laced with mental illness. Listen closely to the voice of God and do not speak doubt. I never said you will not at times feel doubtful, just do not speak it. Remember your flesh is a liar.

Try this test. Tell yourself, "I have a headache." Is your forehead beginning to pound and feel hot? Give it a minute. Now how does it feel? So, you see, you were given power over your flesh from the words you speak. The power of life and death is in the tongue.

Oh, do not forget to bind the headache. Satan has only the amount of control you give him. When you resist Satan, the Holy Spirit is right there to give power to your words and will tell that ol' devil, "I know you heard her, out of here."

Placing God on a time schedule is a form of doubt and distrust. We grow ashamed and distrustful if God does not meet our time schedule (Take it from me, I know.) God help you if the date you told others came and went without the event occurring. Major demon of doubt will join you on your journey. You don't have to invite them; they are party crashers.

I suggest you keep a journal. Write everything down. Not only will what you have written strengthen you spiritually as they come to pass, but it allows you to keep tract of God's personal promises to you. Bless everyone you meet.

Each time you bless someone it comes back to you a hundred fold. The same principle applies, if you curse some one. Evil thoughts will come; use the Word of God and the power of His Holy Spirit dwelling in you to not cross the line. Rather only allow good words to be released into the atmosphere from your lips.

Look back on your life, has not everything you have said come to pass? Your purpose never lost its value. Bless the earth, bless the earth, and bless the earth.

At the Cross, we were redeemed; the price is already paid in full for every evil you've suffered at the hands of others. Pray to not allow the past to cloud your future: Remember Satan uses us against each another. Jesus was wounded and crushed for our sins. He was beaten that we might have peace. He was whipped and we were healed. Isaiah 54:10 says, "For the mountains shall depart, and the hills be removed; but my kindness shall not depart from thee, neither shall the covenant of my peace be removed, saith the Lord that has mercy on thee."

As one Bishop told me, and I faithfully share with you, "Truth crushed to the earth will soon rise." The truth is, you are who God says you are, and therefore you must rise. The battle is not over; our Jesus who died shall be satisfied, and earth and heaven will be one.

There is a wonderful verse in a song I love to sing:
Under his wings, oh what precious enjoyment!
There will I hide till life's trials are o'er!
Sheltered, protected, no evil can harm me,
Resting in Jesus, I'm safe ever more!

Daily morning devotions is a must. We are given our instructions one day at a time. You cannot and will not know your instructions or duties for that day, unless you present yourself for that day's instructions. God acts in and through all that we are, after we have heeded His call. You are an ambassador on assignment.

A final crisis is about to hit this earth, and the end of the great controversy. This message is but another attempt of Father Divine to save His daughters. Our fathers trusted in God, and He delivered them (Psalm 22:4).

As the Holy Spirit leads you, practice a life of fasting. There are many resources available to educate us in fasting. There are many methods of fasting. Some things will only come to pass by prayer and fasting. Fasting brings us into a solemn place of peace with the Holy Spirit.

Telling someone you are praying for him or her, and doing it, is the most powerful thing you can do for anyone. Instead of picking up the phone, to receive or share the latest gossip, pray. Practice a life of prayer. You can pray anywhere you are. Dialoging with the Divine is something you can do all the time, with your mouth shut, and your eyes open.

Keep your promises. If you say something and you don't do it, you are a liar. It is important to remember at all times the character of God: Never forget, "We worship Him in truth and in spirit." If you talk too much, keeping your promises can become rather costly (trust me). Be confident, like David, that you will see the goodness of the Lord in the land of the living.

When life's greater questions come, and they will, be prepared to testify, that of all possibilities, "none but Christ will satisfy."

Overcome a critical spirit. When you are called to service, and if you are reading this message you have been called, you cannot encourage a critical spirit. After every revelation and any manifestation of the Spirit of God in your life, a spirit of criticism may come knocking. Don't answer the door to criticism. Remember, the demons don't wait for an invitation. As you grow in faith, God will receive glory, and you will have His joy.

Guard your anointing carefully. The anointing of God is the most important gift your Father can entrust you with. The more radically a man commits himself to God's kingdom, the greater measure of the kingdom that will be supplied and the more that will shine forth from his life. This demonstrates the fact that God is no respecter of persons; the intensity of the kingdom shining from one's life is in direct proportion to their degree of obedience. Always remember, that our lives are God's Word in action. As you become obedient to God's directions, He will reward you mightily. Every act of obedience is greatly rewarded. As you are obedient to the directions of the Holy Spirit, you will be granted greater responsibilities.

In order to gain God's perspective, you must answer that upward call, and it does not come without sacrifice. You can no longer hide in the crowd when you gain God's perspective. Allow the Holy Spirit to open the door for effective service instead of focusing on the adversaries who oppose you. You must become proactive instead of reactive. Serve without a motive or an underlying agenda to use God for riches. Keep your motive pure and clean, reflective of a heart to share God's love!

You're the one who knows rejection, abandonment, abuse, the odd ball in the family, strange in the head, and yet God sees the value in you and chooses you to become the corner stone. Do not become anxious. When an individual has the call of God on their lives, it takes a while to find out where you fit. We have to find our comfort zone, and live in it. (I warn you, though, don't get too comfortable as God continues to walk us higher and higher into His sovereignty).

At the end of your journey hope will be there. It is our confident assurance that what we hope for will happen. There are no endings, only new beginnings.

Be of good courage, all ye that hope in the Lord, and He will strengthen your heart. Faith is the catalyst for the release of the dynamic power of the Holy Spirit in your life. Catalyst is, an agent that provokes or speeds significant change or action.

Like Mike Murdock sings, in God's presence we are always changed. When the Holy Spirit speaks and we quickly obey, in His presence we are always changed. Surrender your whole body to God, your heart, your mind, your eyes, your ears, your nose, and oh yes, your tongue. Pray for sanctification of the tongue, you know how we are.

Comfort speaks, "**Come as you are**." Don't wait another moment. Just make a decision and say, "Yes, Lord." Right now all that is asked of you is for you to make the decision to answer His call for your life. Make the decision and rest for tonight.

> *Many sorrows shall be to the wicked. But the daughter that trusted in the Lord, mercy shall compass her about.*
>
> (Psalm 32:10)

You will be instructed and taught in the way you should go. Mother Divine will guide you with her eyes. Also, talking too much generates fear, and it does not change the facts. Whenever you get too excited, and you find you are talking much too much about your experiences. Please stop and take notice and correct yourself by sharing more of the Word of Life. By so doing, you serve God in helping humankind to awaken to the life in God's Word.

Assurance fosters health. The assurance of God's approval will promote physical health. Assurance fortifies the soul against doubt, perplexity, and excessive grief. These physical ailments sap the vital forces and induce nervous diseases. Your deliverance from ailments lies within your purpose. Within your purpose lies your authority to have dominion over sickness and death. If you are sick and dying, and you know that you have not fulfilled your purpose or your purpose has not been revealed to you, seek God for a revelation of your purpose and do it.

The use of the Name of Jesus is most effective when used by you under His authority. After your husband takes you as his wife, you have his authority to use his name, and even to cash his checks. When we unconditionally surrender to the Holy Spirit, he gives us the authority to use the name of Jesus, and yes, to cash His checks or expect fulfillment of His promises. If you don't have His authority the check will not clear and I have bounced around enough in this life to know this experience.

Never co-sign for anyone; it is the trap of the enemy. You become a slave to that person. Remember, the wicked borrow and do not repay. Through wisdom is a house built; and by understanding it is established.

As I was experiencing this dark time in my life, I noticed that the darker my night became, the more dirty my home got. I just could not seem to get the energy or the will to clean. The only thing I could do was look at the mess and cry. One day I was in the bathroom taking a shower, and I thought I am anointed, before I realized it, I was saying, "In the name of Jesus, clean."

The Holy Spirit said, **"Antoinette, I am not here to do the things you are capable of doing, only the things that you are not capable of."** What could I do but laugh.

The Holy Spirit can use the condition of our physical homes to make plain to us the condition of our spiritual homes, the heart. No denial here! You cannot command the heart to clean itself; you cannot employ someone to clean for you that which requires a tightly knitted relationship with our Redeemer. The cleaning of the soul is about you and the Holy Spirit. Not the Holy Spirit alone because He is not a party crasher and will patiently await your asking Him to come into your heart. Neither is it just you because in His image, we require the power of His Holy Spirit for a true relationship. This relationship begins the job and brings it to the finish designed by God.

You do not need anyone else's permission to get started. The path is narrow; you must go it alone. It does not matter how anointed someone else is they cannot go with you. Mother Divine will send you landmarks in the form of messengers along your path to destiny. Again, many have traveled that same road, and guess what, they arrived safely.

The Drawing Cords of Love

As Jehovah is holy,
He requires his people to be holy, pure, undefiled.
For without holiness no man shall see the Lord.
Those who worship him in sincerity and truth,
Will be accepted by Him.
Let us all be drawn together with the cords of divine love.
Stay without offense.
Allow the path of healing to lead you to full restoration.

A dream for thought ...

My youngest son, Kemyoe and I were on a highway going home, and we got lost. We found ourselves in this beautiful looking village, but no one could be trusted. Even the people who looked honest and harmless tried to harm us by giving us wrong directions.

We met an old lady looking rather beat up. Every time she talked her tooth would fall out. She told us where to go to get back on the highway. I totally ignored her and listened to the nice lady standing next to her; of course we were still lost. Finally, I decided to try the path the funny looking lady pointed out, and sure enough the path took us to the outer streets of the village, leading us to the highway.

When we arrived at the last house, a young lady working in her garden told us to go straight ahead She said, "The ground looks dangerous, but keep walking straight ahead." She said that we should not go through the park. There were fierce looking animals where we had to walk. It looked like we would surely be eaten alive, or we would definitely be harmed unless we disobeyed and walked through the park. We decided to obey. As we approached each fierce looking animal, it would open its mouth and show us sharp teeth seething with saliva dripping all over the place. Some of the saliva dripped onto our clothes. Amazingly, as we got within a few inches of the animals, they would just get up and walk away. I shouted to the young lady, asking her what we should do when we got to the end of the brown weird path we were walking on. She yelled out I already had the instructions; but I had left them with her.

I remembered at her house, I queried her about her father, having heard he was a bad man with many wives. In stopping to speak with her I forgot my instructions. Quickly, she ran to meet me, and I retrieved my cell phone. She said I would be told what to do: "Just listen." When she gave me my phone, it was singing, "Anywhere with Jesus I can safely go."

The path we walked looked like it would sink at any moment. Nothing along this path reflected God's expected stability. Instead, the surface wobbled like soft jelly. "Just listen." Why in the world should my precious child and I find ourselves alone, here in this strange place and how much could God require of me to place my son in such danger. *Please God, give me courage to listen and obey. Oh yes, I can hear Your voice.* Now, the peace of God began to bolster me and I took my child's hand and pressed forward.

The instant we stepped out, that wobbly foundation solidified. It became solid when our feet touched it.

In comparison, the park seemed safe and strong. Young men dribbled basketballs and others gathered to have fun running around its beautiful landscape. The surface was indeed strong and hard; ever so inviting as a safe place. Yet, as we approached the end of the path we traveled in obedience, suddenly we were back on the right highway. Simple obedience (in hindsight) brought us to a well-lit path in God's order. I could not understand how we got to the highway that quickly, because there were miles and miles of an open field before us while we were traveling. As soon as our feet touched the highway, we were back in our car, and the navigation system came on.

Where was this navigation system when we needed it? It was still in the car; the car never left the highway, but we did. We were on our way home again, headed in the right direction. *Thank You, Father, for restoring us, leading us back into Your righteous order, when we find ourselves off course.*

As you embark upon this journey to the Mother Divine, keep your eyes on the Navigator.

CHAPTER ELEVEN

Raised as a Baton

My peace I leave with you,
My peace I give unto you,
Not as the world giveth, give I unto you,
Let not your heart be troubled,
Neither let it be afraid.

April 11, 2005, and it is twenty minutes past 4 o'clock in the afternoon.

So, I am being raised as a baton. I have been cleaned, shaped, polished and sent. Sent where? Where do I go from here? Please don't tell me that I am an inactive baton. I have been prepared and now I am being placed on a shelf to collect dust! An unused baton, oh boy! That I don't think I could survive. I have to be busy, and about my Father's business. What are my instructions? Where do I go from here? I must be busy if I am not asleep. Somebody please listen. I am not sleeping. What do I do now? My soul is growing. How does 4 years old sound? Please give me an assignment. I won't talk too much. I can now listen; my ears, they know how to listen.

"Antoinette, this is your Abba Father Divine."

Yes, Father Divine.

"Why are you so afraid? Why do you keep running? Are you having a problem seeing and accepting who you are? Are you afraid of your own power, and what I created when I created you?"

Yes, Father Divine, I am. (Wow, another pimple here...) I don't know why I am afraid to be quiet. I thought I overcame this fear. If I am not sleeping, I have to be active. I just cannot stand being still. This time I am not afraid to know what was done to me. Although I am afraid of the revelation of who I am.

Who am I? Really, I want to know, but don't know how to just allow You to show me. I call my friends to get away from the revelation, and they have all suddenly begun speaking prophetically. What is going on here?

"Antoinette, I need you to get back to basics. Enjoy where you are. Glean every aspect of the presence of Comfort. There is so much more about Her that She has yet to show you. I miss your early morning appointments with Me. I miss your worship. To remain delivered, you must stay closely connected to Me. You will always need me to stay on the heights that you will be taken. I will never leave you or forsake you. You must never leave Me nor forsake Me. I have always loved you and will always protect you. Don't be afraid."

I won't.

"After every revelation comes a time of depression, or what would feel like a depression. The physical body is drained; therefore, you must be filled up again for another journey. At the end of each journey, there is always the beginning of another. There are never endings, only beginnings. I required you to have rest and to walk refreshed and refilled to continue. Yesterday's anointing will not protect you against tomorrow's trials and obstacles that you must overcome. Every season needs a fresh release of my anointing, and a daily out-pouring to keep and hold you. So, My dear, allow Me to refill you with the power of My Holy Spirit."

I will. Since You have spoken Your desire that I have rest, can I tell You how exhausted I am and thank You for allowing me to rest in You? I am going to rest a bit, and then get my physical house in order. Can't seem to get back to basics without order. That is really going to be a job. Father Divine, is it okay to hire someone to assist me with bringing order and cleanliness into my home? Not that I am not humble, I am just so tired.

"Yes, Antoinette."

I really wish I could sleep. I have not really slept in about three weeks. The chaos in my soul won't allow my body to rest. "Please, God, help this lonely heart to find stillness in Your wholeness."

If I fall asleep, I might be too tired to wake up. I am tempted to call my friends, though I realize this is a personal journey for me, as they will just tell me to stop writing and get some sleep. They are really beginning to sound like Your tape recorders. I would really welcome a visit from Rest Divine. I never knew falling asleep could become such a difficult task. I am trying so hard to relax.

My family sits downstairs laughing and having a good time, going on with life, as if nothing major is happening, oblivious to the transformation of their matriarch taking place under this roof. Perhaps, they will conclude that I am a basket case, (if only they knew). Or don't they care? The talking and laughing is so loud, can't they whisper? They are probably thinking – the happier we are the crazier she will feel. Let her rot upstairs. Oh Father, what am I thinking?

This abuse of my soul can only mean the enemy looms within distance of what we are working through here, as godly order will soon ascend upon me and in this house. Such an attack to thwart my freedom and purpose: Why else such a major attack of the mind? Where did those thoughts come from? I desperately need a visit from Rest Divine.

Please, I need You now, I don't have the strength to deal with one of those silent treatments. I am really losing it here. My blanket smells like ranch-flavored nachos. Please don't tell me I want to eat my blanket. I could use one of those spiritual sleeping pills right about now.

"Antoinette, even though you are very tired, you are being quiet. You don't need a spiritual sleeping tablet, that's only needed when you are talking too much."

When will You and I ever agree on anything? What do I need to rest?

"Peace."

Peace? Where is Peace? And how do I find it?

"My peace I leave with you. My peace I give unto you; not as the world giveth, give I unto you; let not your heart be troubled, neither let it be afraid. Let not your heart be troubled, if ye believe in God, ye believe also in Me. In my father's house are many mansions, if it were not so, I would have told you. I go and prepare a place for you, and if I go and prepare a place for you, I will come again, and receive you unto Myself, that where I am there ye may be also."

I really thought I had cried the last teardrop, and now You have started a whole new section. When do you ever stop?

"I will never stop, Antoinette, until all my children are home. I miss My daughters and sons so much. I experience the same pain you do when your children are snatched away from you. I will do whatever it takes, and use whoever will allow Me to get My children home."

You would even use an exhausted baton?

"I would use an exhausted baton, Antoinette. But, I will uphold you with my strength. To whom much is given, much is required."

I understand. I will lovingly serve You, Father Divine, with every tool You have given me. Just tell me what to do, lest You replace me with a rock. Yes, I read where you said, if I refuse to praise You, You have the power to make the rocks cry out Your praises.

"Antoinette, you are in the stage of infancy. You just got here. Enjoy the relief, the solitude, and the rest. That is usually what babies do at this stage of life. Don't try to lead Me, allow Me to lead you. Babies need their mother's protection to survive, allow Me to

mother you. Also, I need to enjoy My newborn daughter, so please, drink the milk you are being fed. It isn't time for you to be fed cereal. Enjoy the stage you are in, Antoinette; remember, just milk and please stop complaining."

Oh!

"Complaining isn't caring for the soul. For the soul to be renewed your thought patterns must change. Your soul longs to be free, but it can only do so once you cultivate and nourish the soil of your heart with thoughts of love, joy, peace, and happiness. You can force your body to do the things it doesn't want to, but you cannot force the soul. Your soul knows when it is safe for it to evolve. The evil thoughts you allow, the self-hatred and condemnation are the bars used by Satan to hold the soul a prisoner. When the soul is free, Antoinette, you experience total freedom and joy. Not just for fleeting moments, but a lifetime of complete happiness. Allow Me to free your soul."

Yes, Father Divine, please free my soul completely. I cannot express the desire I feel when I think of total freedom, because such an experience is unknown to me. But my soul is so excited with anticipation. I long for Your healing touch, so it can break the chains holding me captive. My soul longs to breathe, to escape from this darkness. This festering pain has been locked away much too long. Now that my soul acknowledges it has a purpose, it will not lay dormant any longer. The years of my soul being silent are now past, my soul has a voice, a voice that will be heard. My soul is unique, powerful, and gifted, indeed a force for God that will shake heaven and hell. I have a name. I have an identity.

I have a purpose, a God-ordained purpose, and that purpose is who I am. I am not a dirty piece of rag like the devil would have me to believe, but a jewel, a valued daughter of God mirroring His Love to others. Satan will regret the evil he has done to me, for what he meant for my harm, truly God is using for my highest good and His glory. I choose right now to forgive the people so easily besieged by evil and was used like silly-putty in the hands of Satan. They, like me were fooled, and indeed were blinded by a formidable foe, the devil.

I know many did not understand why they treated me the way they did. I know I did not understand why I treated some the way I did. To those I have wronged, please forgive me. I would want to believe right now, that because I was victimized, I had the right to hurt others; but I did not, and still do not have that right. A wounded and hurting daughter can only wound and hurt others. Even our good intentions have an evil motive, so I know that there are many scarred by wounds and hurt by my good and evil actions. I will not find an excuse for the evil actions or reactions of my broken heart; I can only ask your forgiveness.

My apologies to the souls hurt by the necessary truth desperately needed to free my soul. My motive has never been to hurt, but to heal. My soul would not allow any compromise; it would only accept its freedom based on truth. You too can free your soul by telling your truth. With our souls freed, we can enjoy true love, trust, and fellowship. Allow the freedom of my soul to encourage you to be true to yourself, to lead you into a new way to view life. The possibilities are endless when the soul is free.

To be free to soar like an eagle is a goal worth fighting for. To have freedom is wonderful, and is a way of life the human mind left to its own could never comprehend nor achieve. You have to experience it to believe it. But it is oh, so real.

I remember Kathy saying that we can start living in Heaven right here on earth. Now I am beginning to understand exactly what she was talking about. It is the same love, joy, and peace that must now be cultivated in our hearts. The Holy Angels of God will not wait at Heaven's gate to lay hands on you; the development of Christ's character reflected in us begins now. The only thing we will take with us to heaven is our salvation enriched by godly character. If your character is evil, only Satan has room for you in Hotel Hell; if your character reflects righteousness, God has a house filled with many mansions prepared for you. Righteousness is decency, uprightness, integrity and walking in the order of God. It is not perfection, as all have sinned and come short of the glory of God. Yet, it is a perfect heart, pliable and anxious to absorb the power of God's Holy Spirit to work His will into our lives. With repentance we surrender to the sacrifice of the cross. Not only will we make right decisions in all things, we will have the right motive. Only then will the reflection in our mirror of life show righteousness reflected in right doing; both the action and the motive will be right. We will never understand or accept the redemptive work of the cross until we are ready to face our truth. Those locked in dark rooms commit suicide. Others, in their relentless quest for peace and order, self-medicate and become drug addicts. Some prostitute their bodies because they fail to see themselves in the image of God, and low self-esteem is the work of the enemy. And then, some turn to alcohol because they do not understand who they are. Because of being made in the image of God, they cannot face who they are and what has been done to them. All evidence points to the fact that they are so removed from the divine image of God. That, my friend, is the sacrifice of the cross, the covering and removal of your past sin.

Our Father has a diary, and a set time to return for His children. Do not allow the price paid for your salvation to go to waste. You are required only to simply choose God, and allow Him to nurture, protect, and lead you all the way. Our Father Divine will always keep His eyes on you. He will lead and teach you in the way you should go. *Father Divine, I now give to You all my evil ways and selfish habits; the traits within me that do not reflect Your character, I give them to You in the Name of Jesus. I want to represent You in such a way that would confuse Satan. He will not know if he is in the presence of Jesus Himself or one of His daughters.*

I have a desire in my heart, a desire to step on Satan's head. The enmity I have for him is the enmity I know my Father Divine must have for him too. I have been raised as a warrior in the army of the Lord, so Satan you had better look out! I only need my assignment, and you are *outta* here. Father Divine, I sense a warrior spirit arising within me. What is happening?

"It has been revealed to you some of the things Satan has done to you. It is okay to be angry about the sins of your enemy. Be angry enough for Me to anoint you with a warrior spirit. This war is not against flesh and blood, but against principalities, against spiritual wickedness in high places. You need the protecting anointing of God to keep you safe on the battlefield. The war for souls is fierce. To become victorious we must allow King Jesus to fight our battles for us. My Son has never lost a battle yet. Sometimes He makes decisions that might appear not to be in our favor, but if we always keep in mind that all things work together for good to them Who love God, and are called according to His purpose."

I am on the battlefield for my Lord,
I am on the battlefield for my Lord.
You know I promise Him that I,
I would serve Him til I die,
I am on the battlefield for my Lord.

I need You to love me, Mother Divine, to caress and cuddle me. I need to feel the warmth of Your presence. I just need to know that You are here with me, right now. I really miss You. Where is Peace Divine? I really want to speak to Him. Maybe tomorrow; I want to know You, Peace Divine.

April 12, 2005, and it is forty-five minutes past the hour of 9 o'clock in the morning.

"Good morning, Antoinette."

Good morning, Holy Spirit.

"You said last night you wanted to meet Peace Divine. Well, I am here. You purchased a book about a year ago written by Iyanla Vanzant, called *Faith in the Valley*. When you purchased that book you

wondered why you bought it when you had so many unread books. I knew that the time was fast approaching when you would need the instructions given to My daughter written within that book. Find the book. There you will find vital lessons recorded for daughters on the journey to Peace. You have now embarked upon your journey to Peace. My Peace I leave with you, My Peace I give unto you, Not as the world giveth, Give I unto you, Let not your heart be troubled, Neither let it be afraid."

Thank You, Peace Divine. I welcome You, Peace Divine. May I be at peace and my heart remain open. May I awaken to the light of my own true nature to grow while accepting your healing to become a source of healing to others. I welcome You, Peace Divine. I was not aware I had memorized this prayer from years ago. Thank You for Your awesome presence here, Peace Divine, and I pray that You will stay with me. Fill me with Your peace, Your peace that surpasseth all understanding. Completely wrap my soul in Your peace.

"Antoinette, you always pray that I stay with you. Know that I have never left you nor ever will. I will be with you always."

I just had a thought, tell me if I am wrong. Kathy Spaar was chosen to usher me into the presence of Comfort Divine, and Iyanla Vanzant's writing was used to teach me how to enter the presence of Peace?

"Yes, Antoinette."

My sister, Iyanla, is she aware she is a chosen daughter, who will teach her sisters how to enter the presence of Peace Divine?

"If she doesn't, she's about to find out."

I hope someday I will get a chance to meet my sister Iyanla in person.

"Antoinette, right now I need you to read her writings. Let the anointing of her words usher you into the presence of Peace Divine."

You know something, Peace Divine, since I first believed that Part 1 of this manuscript was complete, I believe around April 8, 2005 I have ceased from crying. The need to cry continues to haunt me, but there are no tears. Isn't that something? I can't believe I have not cried for so many days. I am beginning to think the preparation was worth every moment of suffering. Relief: The realization that I have not cried for four entire days makes me want to cry for joy. Don't worry, I won't cry. If I did it would be a weird looking dry cry, as my soul has emptied itself of sorrow and hopelessness, leaving me with no tears. Perhaps I should dance for You? Yes, I can honor You with a dance.

"Antoinette, did you start reading the book?"

No!

"Antoinette, obedience is absolutely necessary as you are ushered into every aspect of my character. As your soul matures, your flesh will war against you; it must be brought under subjection, disciplined into the newness of your life."

I am sorry. I will begin immediately. I can hardly wait to meet You, Peace Divine. I hope I can recognize You. How will I know You?

"Antoinette!"

Okay, reading. I am reading. No more writing tonight, I will read.

Chapter Twelve

Peace. Ya Lordi!

Morning has broken, like the first morning
Blackbird has spoken, like the first bird
Praise for the singing, praise for the morning
Praise for them springing fresh from the world

Sweet the rain's new fall, sunlit from heaven
Like the first dewfall, on the first grass
Praise for the sweetness of the wet garden
Sprung in completeness where his feet pass

Mine is the sunlight, mine is the morning
Born of the one light, Eden saw play
Praise with elation, praise every morning
God's recreation of the new day

Cat Stevens

April 13, 2005, and it is six o'clock in the morning.

Peace Divine, I am in the shower attempting to get it together; I must venture out to work today. Suddenly the shower door opens, and in walks this beautiful son of Yours. He takes me in his arms and says, "I love you, sweetheart, and I always will; please don't forget that." I kept looking at him. Is this for real? Or am I really losing my mind? My CD player started playing and Juanita Bynum was singing, "Peace, my peace, You're my peace. The kind of Peace that passeth all understanding When I should be crying, When I should be filled with despair, When my back is up against the wall, Receive God's peace in your heart, in your soul."

The anointing of Your peace now fills my soul. Ya Lordi! Thank You.

Peace Divine, does my husband represent peace? Or is it because he seems to have a piece for me? Am I becoming confused here? My God, is he laying me on the bed? I am not on the floor. Is this really happening? I am trying to think, I am trying to understand. *Oh, the sanctity of marriage can sometimes take you down a long, lonely road in the darkness of the night.* You know what, Peace Divine? We will talk about this later. I would sometimes run away from Comfort, but I choose to spend a while with Peace. Ya Lordi!

So, not only am I underdeveloped, I am untrained in the spiritual virtue of Peace. Peace might have been in my life for a very long time, and I did not recognize him. (Is this possible?) Peace appeared to be dark, cold, and always angry. Or, am I the one who has always encouraged a dark, cold, and angry atmosphere? What is going on here? Am I the problem? Or, was Peace and I used to war against each other? Peace Divine, I hope you will tolerate my questions the way Comfort did. I have been taught that no question is a foolish question. I do ask a lot of questions, but it's the way I learn.

"It's okay, Antoinette, Comfort told me all about you."

Peace Divine, why didn't I recognize You before now? Comfort was with me through my weeping, healing, and restoration. If I am restored, where do You fit in?

"Antoinette, you are being raised as a baton, your preparation isn't over. Raised does not mean sent. After your seasons of weeping and healing, your soul was restored to God's original plan. I can only enter and dwell permanently in a restored vessel. When I abide in your soul, I am there to stay.

"Now that I have come, your heart will no longer be troubled; neither will you be afraid."

Are You serious? I will no longer be afraid? What do I say here?

"You don't have to say anything, Antoinette. I have a quiet disposition. You don't speak peace, you live peace."

But Comfort thinks I talk too much. How can I live in peace if I talk so much?

"Yes, you did Antoinette. But talking was a trait your Father Divine allowed to help you deal with the pain that housed your soul. That is why I am being ushered into your soul after restoration. To live in peace, you will be taught to develop a less talkative nature."

I don't know how to be peaceful and quiet at the same time.

"Antoinette, being busy all the time, even within My service is not being peaceful. Being peaceful is that wonderful assurance My children possess in the calm and storms of life."

So, what do I have to do?

"Nothing, I will teach you."

Okay.

"Antoinette, My peace is not as the world giveth. Allow My peace, the peace of your Father, to come into your heart right now."

I welcome You, Peace Divine.

I welcome You into my heart,

I welcome You into my soul,

I welcome You into spirit.

Occupy my temple forever.

"Thank you, Antoinette for allowing Me into your life."

No, I thank You for re-conceiving me. Now, I'm born again.

"Antoinette, your peace is in realizing your Father's purpose for your life. After the restoration of your soul, you possess the dominion and all the authority that was originally yours. Your Father now has no secrets from you. Your peace is not disturbed by the events or process of any given situation, because you would have already been shown the end results. Satan can only confuse the process, he cannot change the end results or your Father's plan for you.

"There isn't much that has happened in your life that you weren't aware of the end results. This lack of peace came from not trusting or understanding who you are because of Me. I am in you. Now that you are beginning to understand the authority and power within you, there is no reason to allow your peace to be taken from you."

I understand. Peace Divine, I have often wondered, if Satan no longer has access to heaven where does his knowledge of your having dispatched angels with an answer to our prayers come from? Or, when a blessing has been sent to us? He always seems to be able to barge in with some conflicting message right before your Holy Messengers. You know the experiences I am thinking about. Just before every message of comfort, he sneaks in with a chest-thumping message of fear. I need to understand how he functions to keep this thief from stealing my peace.

The spiritual virtue Peace is so important to me right now. I value You, Peace Divine, I don't ever want You to leave me.

"Antoinette, there are many things you will not quite understand at this point, but be assured what was said to the children of Israel in Exodus 14:13-14 is being said this day to you, 'Don't be afraid. Just stand where you are and watch; I will rescue you.' The enemy that you see today will become powerless by My power and the Holy Spirit itself working in you. I, the Lord, will fight for you. You won't have to lift a finger in your defense. My child, your enemy Satan has no power or control except that which I allow. You have My confident assurance that I will never leave you nor forsake you.

Antoinette, I bring you now to the place to bid goodbye to your past. When you welcomed Me into your heart, your life in your Father began. Saying so long to the past, and welcoming the unknown is never easy. Your actions, thoughts and behaviors will now demonstrate the transformed you, not the old Antoinette who was born into sin, being shapened in iniquity. You must begin to live as a light created to bring comfort into this world. The salt of all the tears you have shed has seasoned the earth. The past, the tears, all the pain you endured, was necessary for the souls waiting now for comfort."

May I sing unto You, Father Divine?

I've got peace like a river,

I've got peace like a river,

I've got peace like a river, in my soul.

I've got peace like a river.

I've got peace like a river.

I've got peace like a river, in my soul.

Thank You, Father.

"I needed you to endure all the things you have been through. You have been persevered by My grace. Now, allow Me to season the earth with the salt of your tears. In order for Peace Divine to take full residence in your life, complete trust is a requirement. Walking into the unknown requires the gifts of Peace and Trust for survival. Peace can only dwell in trust. You are being greatly rewarded My daughter, for your obedience through all your tears. You have done well."

Thank You.

"Antoinette, there will be a lot of shifting going on in your life during this period of preparation. Do not be alarmed; it is important

that you trust Me. Listen closely for My voice only. There is a lot in your life that has to be removed; there is so much more to be added to your life. Just be aware that all things will work together for your good, because you love your Father."

Peace Divine, I am feeling so much pain right now. I can hardly breathe. What is going on here? The pain involved in saying farewell chokes me, but I choose now to say goodbye to my past, and welcome my future.

<u>April 14, 2005</u>, and it is seven minutes past eight o'clock in the evening.

How do I describe the pain of saying goodbye, even when the past was hurtful? It hurts sounds so lame. Why is it hurting so much to say good-bye to a very painful and abusive past? Is the unknown that scary? Is my trust in You wavering already? I really do not understand. Right now I am thinking that I should feel ever so happy, soaring like an eagle as I have waited on You, jumping hoops and feeling like a kid in a candy store, but instead another kind of pain is trying to swallow me.

I really can't breathe.

I am suffocating.

Is this the experience of a newborn about to leave the comfort of his mother's womb and enter the world for the first time, afraid of the unfamiliar? Is this birth premature? What is going on now? I would really love to cry right now, but is it safe to cry? I feel like my bottom is been slapped, and there's a host of angels calmly waiting on me to breathe, knowing full well I am travailing through this birthing channel to the newness of life in You, Father. They simply wait, "Is she breathing yet?"

Suddenly, there are shouts of joy, laughter and dance: "Looks like she made it! She's breathing." Exclaiming, "All that she will need she has; her ten fingers and toes." Dare they ask, "Is she normal?" For we know that all things work together for good for those who love the Lord and for those who are the called according to His purpose in Heaven (Romans 8:28).

I'm birthed again after being re-conceived and, most importantly, I am in His image. Let the angels rejoice!

Chapter Thirteen

Coming Out of the Valley

We've come this far by faith,
Leaning on the Lord.
Trusting in His Holy Word.
He's never failed me yet.
I say, Oh, Oh, Oh,
Can't turn around,
We've come this far by faith.[2]

April 15, 2005, and it is ten o'clock in the morning.

Perhaps Marie can assist me, as my session with her is about to begin.

"Antoinette, you have entered the valley of saying goodbye to your past. I am thinking, this sounds quite familiar. Remember, we discussed goodbye is extremely difficult. The same principles apply to your soul. Your soul is saying goodbye to the familiar, the comfortable, and the known. It is not an easy process. But, you can do this; you have made it this far. The worst of your suffering is over. The labor pain subsides, lessening the intensity of your pain. There is far less pain, even though it may seem to feel much worse. You are experiencing the triggering of the nerves."

"The baby is here."

"You are here."

I am born again.

---

[2]Traditional Gospel, *"We've Come This Far by Faith"*

"Remember, everything you are going through is absolutely necessary. The integration of your revealed past, and the revelation of your future, is a requirement needed by the soul for it to evolve. So in the midst of the depression, rejoice. You are finally here."

"Your nostrils have been cleared of the umbilical fluids."

"A brand new baby girl, Mother Divine's daughter."

"It is safe to breathe, Antoinette."

How did She know I could not breathe?

"Antoinette, you are very quiet. Are you okay?"

Yes, Marie, I am just listening to you."

"Antoinette, take a break from all this. Go out and do something nice for yourself." Like what? I am thinking; I have no idea what I enjoy. Oh Lord! I have no idea what would make me happy. "Don't worry, My dear, Mother Divine will show you."

Okay.

April 15...LATER IN THE DAY...It is now seventeen minutes past one o'clock in the afternoon.

"Antoinette."

Yes, Peace Divine.

"You are powerless to change your past, and you are powerless to decide your future. All you need to do is live in this moment. When given choices, and they will come, remember you are empowered by My Spirit and if you seek wisdom, you will make responsible decisions. As a newborn, your duty right now is to be relieved, to enjoy the solitude, and to rest. All that is required of a new baby is to rest, feed, and grow."

Okay.

Own only what you can carry with you; know language, know countries, know people. Let your memory be your travel bag.

-Alexander Solzhenitsyn

April 15...LATER IN THE DAY...It is now six o'clock in the evening.

Driving home from work, I thought, Jesus gave up His divinity to become humanity. What did comfort and peace cost me? Nothing. He took my nothing, and recreated something. I am now my Father's child, created in His image.

I spoke to one of my friends earlier today. Having received some rather bad news, I knew firsthand her pain. I felt her devastation. Yet, somehow in the midst of it all, I was able to smile. How had I learned to smile? Because I remembered when I was the one distraught, with little hope of overcoming such horrid circumstances, and did not believe I could ever make it through. Well, I did.

I know my friend will make it. While being prepared for my journey, it seems there were not many people who were there for me consistently, but I'll be there for her. Speak to me, Father, as I lend her a consistent shoulder; and lead me not into the temptation to interfere with Your ultimate plan for her life. Her expectations must come from You. Yet, however Your Holy Spirit leads me, I will warn her of Satan's traps, so she can avoid them. She will become a force for God graced through these difficulties to shake heaven and hell.

I don't know what happened, Peace Divine, but I was on the phone with my best friend Blondell. She mentioned something happening in a mutual friend's life. How do I explain what happened except the conversation triggered something within me, and I went off on my friend. I felt like I was going insane. I said so many unkind things to my friend. I verbalized such words of hate and anger that I did not even know still existed within me, and they were definitely being directed at the wrong person. She listened, as only an obedient servant and good sister could.

Oh God, what did I do?

Blondell is my best friend; she did not deserve what I just did.

What did I do? What is happening to me? Barely able to constrain myself, I called Blondell back, for not only is she my best friend, she has one of the best hearts walking this earth right now. When she saw I was calling on the line, she picked up the phone and just said, "Baby, I love you. I understood what was happening. I love you unconditionally. I have no plans to push you away or reject you. Satan will not have the victory." She continued, "I never quite understood my purpose, but now I know. I love you even more than I did before we spoke earlier, even though I thought I had already given you all my love, and did not think I could love you any more than I did. We will get through this."

Peace Divine, she did not push me away nor reject me; instead she said she loved me even more. Thank You so much for anointing my friend's heart. She still loves me. She did not throw me away. She did not feel I was defective. She said I would always be her best sister/friend. She still loves me. She said the only thing that has changed, is that she loves me even more. Thank You, Peace Divine.

CHAPTER FOURTEEN

Breaking Old Habits

As the hart panteth after the water brooks, so panteth my soul after Thee, Oh GOD.

(Psalm. 42:1)

"*Get into the habit of saying, 'Speak, LORD,' & Life will become a romance. Every time circumstances press, say, 'Speak, LORD'; make time to listen!*"

(9/4, *My Utmost for HIS Highest Calendar*, Oswald Chambers)

Why am I having such a hard time with this transition? To lose even the perception of control, is something my heart is rejecting right now. Any sign of rejection I sense, I start hurting all over again. I thought with my past and my future purpose revealed to me, things would be a whole lot different. Why does the pain still exist on this side of the journey?

If I am born again to win, why is it hurting so much more than when I entered this world born in sin and shapen in iniquity? I cannot recall any pain with my first birth; none whatsoever.

I am a daughter created in Your image; this seems like quite a lot of suffering for a newborn. It is like I am living all over again, but the pain of being forced out has intensified. What is happening? I don't want to die as a new baby.

I want to survive. I want to grow up. Please do not let me die. I have lost control of everything. Nothing is going my way. My way! My way! My way! The former things I did to stop heart pain, are not working anymore. I don't even have the strength to try them, in fact all of a sudden I can't remember what I used to do. I just have to lie here, and do what? Do what?

Speak to me, Lord. Quiet, my soul, and let me hear Your voice.

"Antoinette, just write."

Just write and do what?

"Just write."

This seems rather cold to me. How about I eat some nachos and get fat?

Get fat, Antoinette.

Shave your head, Antoinette.

Knock out somebody, Antoinette.

Go and check into a mental asylum, Antoinette. Sure feels like I am losing my mind here, and all You can say to me is "Write."

"You are not being forced, Antoinette, you are being taught to listen for My voice just as the deer pants for water. You thirst and hunger for not just My peace, My comfort, but for righteousness. Breathe in and then breathe out. I'm with you."

I was breathing just fine, before all this Mother/Father Divine business started.

"Were you Antoinette? Were you breathing just fine? Are you saying that you don't want to be where you are right now?"

I am not saying all that. I really don't know what I am saying. I just don't like having no control. When I want to sleep, You say, "Stay awake." When I want to eat, You say, "Fast." When I want solid food, You say, "Drink water." When I want to stink, You say, "Take a shower." When I want to talk, You say, "Write."

"Antoinette, would you say that you would know how to survive right now without Me? That you would prefer it if I left you alone."

Isn't that the way You planned it? That we cannot survive without You?

"Were you surviving before, Antoinette? Would you say you were better off?"

No, I would not.

"Then why not trust Me, Antoinette, with the control you seem to think you have or need? Have I disappointed you before?"

Yes, You have.

"Have not what you perceived as a disappointment worked out for your own good?"

Yes, it has.

"Haven't I proved that as My daughter, I will never leave you nor forsake you? Antoinette you said before that you would not want to go through your preparation all over again. In fact, you said you would not do it; but if I had to die all over again for you, I would. If I had to be spat upon all over again for you, I would. If I had to be nailed to that wooden cross all over again for you, I would. If a spear had to be driven in my side all over again for you, I would.

"If I had to leave My father for thirty-three years again for you, I would. If I had to give up My divinity for humanity all over again for you, I would. There is nothing that I would not do all over again for you."

I am so sorry, Peace Divine, please forgive me. Why do I seem to always take a step forward and two steps backward?

"You want to run against My time set aside for you to crawl and

then walk. Remember, you are being re-conceived because of habits you learned while running in circles. Rest, My daughter and let Me carry you in My arms."

Is that what I have been doing? Running in circles?

"Yes, that is what you are doing. Pride and self confidence are not allowed in My service. Loving Me is total dependence and trust in My will for your life. You can trust Me, Antoinette. Release the past; you are safe in My arms. You don't have to take care of yourself, I will take care of you; I will take care of your every need. When your commitment to Me outweighs your commitment to yourself, you shall have the desires of your heart (Psalm 37:4). That is My word to you."

Thank You. I am so sorry for the way I behaved. Abba Father, please forgive me. Abba, Father, please help me to break the old habits and glorify You with obedience.

"You are forgiven. I know and understand what you are going through. Your fight now is for Me."

Thank You, Peace Divine.

"Get some rest, Antoinette, you are very tired."

Peace Divine, we are definitely seeing eye to eye; we are on the same page right about now. I love You.

"I also love you, Antoinette, very much. Remember, though, My thoughts are above you as well as My ways. This is just the beginning."

You said that the way of a parent is to tell a child that they were loved.

"I am your Father; you are My daughter. I am also a parent Who knows how to lead you back to Me if you don't obey My Word. You need to rest."

I give You, Father, my obedience: Your will to become mine.

April 15...A long day and it is now ten o'clock at night.

I rested and slept as commanded. My emotions feel a lot better, but I am still quite tired.

"Antoinette, you have experienced an extreme amount of suffering on this journey and for the abuse you endured, I am sorry. Because you have made it this far, does not mean the side effects of all you have been through will just disappear. Your continued restoration and learning is a process; there is much for you to learn and unlearn. Once you stop resisting My arms, settle down, and stand still for Me to simply love you, there will come new heights for you to gain. There is a lot you have to be taught before you are sent to bring healing to the world. A sent baton must be a balanced baton."

CHAPTER FIFTEEN

Raised as a Baton

April 16, 2005, and it is 16 minutes past 4 o'clock in the evening.

Peace Divine, I am no longer resisting Your arms. I love the protection of Your arms. I have settled down, and am being very quiet for now. My soul said she is now 6 years old; isn't she growing a bit fast?

"Antoinette, your soul cannot enjoy her freedom to its fullest until her healing is complete, and she has the ability to bring others to that place of restoration. She learns quickly. Hearing and applying the things you have learned to your life is called maturing in the things of the Spirit. Your soul have been a prisoner for 41 years physically; she wants to get to 7 years old spiritually, where she will be given all the necessary tools for her new life. Even though she is free, she needs her tools to maintain such freedom and happiness. Her training will continue into eternity, but to accomplish her purpose here on earth, seven is complete to effectively fulfill that purpose. And as they say in your world, "As long as you have your own tools, you will be taught on the job.'"

"More importantly though, is that the redemptive blood of My Son has given you mighty weapons for warfare against an invisible enemy. You are victorious and being prepared for anything or anyone that should come against you."

CHAPTER SIXTEEN

"Beware of Satan's Temptation"

"...and pray to not be led into temptation and to be delivered from all evil."

Dear God, not only are You the keeper of my faith, but You are the lover of my soul. So, I ask You to keep me from failing when You feel it necessary to test me and even to retest me as gold is retested. Help me to know the right thing to do and deliver me from the evil, which awaits Your children in this life. In Jesus' Name. Amen, Amen, and Amen.

"One of Satan's greatest pleasures is to set baits for My children, and to watch them fall blindly into his traps, causing great confusion. He knows your past more accurately than you do; in fact he knows your nature better than you. He can and does trigger fear in your heart through his endless manipulations: Something as simple and seemingly harmless as bringing a color before your eyes will bring back a sad memory causing anxiety or depression. He knows when his baits are most effective to intentionally cause interference in your preparation."

"Remember the experience with Blondell? A bait was laid to trap you; Blondell shared something with you to help you; instead, a single word used by her triggered such an awful reaction from you. Satan can no longer harm you, but he is not above using the painful reminders of your past to cause you much grief. He will use any tool at his disposal."

"Pray daily for the sanctification of your tongue. In tossing out his bait, he can lure you in easily by the sharpness of your tongue. He will use your tongue to reel you back into his trap. He looks for

weakness in you and tempts you relentlessly in his effort to make your life miserable. Be watchful and prayerful every step of the way."

"Your soul is indeed growing beautifully every step of the way. Offense is Satan's great bait for a growing child of God. Psalm 119:165 says, "Great peace have they which love thy law; and nothing shall offend them..." Antoinette, when you are offended the end result is disobedience. I am your Abba Father and I have given you many wonderful gifts. Walk in these gifts and your soul shall surely prosper."

Thank You, Abba Father.

"Listen and hear My voice. Know Me. Know My dear one, you will not be judged by your gifts; they were given to you freely. You will be judged, Antoinette, by the fruits of the Spirit cultivated in your life. The results; cultivated in your life is the character of Christ Himself."

The fruits of the Spirit can be found in Galatians 5:22-23. They are:

Love;

Strong affection for another arising out of kinship or personalities;

Warm attachment; enthusiasm or devotion;

The fatherly concern of God for humankind;

Brotherly concern for others;

A person's adoration of God;

Joy;

A state of happiness or felicity;

Bliss;

A source or cause of delight;

The emotion evoked by well-being;

Success; or good fortune or by the prospect of possibility of one's desires.

Peace;

At Peace;

A state of tranquility or quietness;

Freedom from oppressive thoughts or emotions;

In a state of harmony;

Patience;

The capacity, habit, or fact of being patient;

Solitaire;

Kindness - A kind deed;

Favor;

The quality or state of being kind;

Archaic;

Affection;

Goodness - The quality or state of being good; the nutritious, flavorful, or beneficial part of something;

Faithfulness - Faithful;

Loyal;

Constant;

Staunch;

Steadfast; a steady and unwavering course in love, allegiance or conviction;

Resolute;

Gentleness - The quality or state of being gentle; mildness of manners or disposition;

Self-control - Restraint exercised over one's own impulses, emotions or decisions.

"When the Holy Spirit is working in us, the mighty providence of God is always working outside of us in perfect correspondence and preparation."

Chapter Seventeen

Abandoned to God

The Source of my Feminine Power

April 18, 2005, and it is twenty minutes past nine o'clock in the morning.

When the heart sees what God wants it to see, the response must come with a willingness to spend and to be spent for God's purpose. The willingness to spend and to be spent is to say goodbye to the past. Abandoned to God.

April 19, 2005, and it is half past the hour of eleven o'clock in the morning.

While speaking to a sister/friend today, she shared with me the struggles in her experience leading her to a closer walk with God as He called her into service. I shared with her that there was no way God would take us to the next level without total trust and dependence on Him. As I shared with her I realized I was guilty of doing exactly the same thing to God. While being prepared for His purpose, I complained every step of the way.

How I pray to never regress again; by God's grace I am sure going to try real hard. My goal is to be completely honest about my struggles as I travel to the heart of Mother Divine; and my struggles have indeed been countless. Total trust is the condition for Peace Divine to occupy or dwell in the soul.

CHAPTER EIGHTEEN

"Twenty-four Hours Before You"

April 20, 2005 and it is twenty-five minutes before the hour of ten o'clock in the morning.

I am on my way to Sanctuary Retreat again. Wisdom Divine, the thread spinning out of my feminine core pressing me into a divine place of solitude and tranquility. Such resolve to live in God's peace. My soul's desire for this path of my journey being traveled is to find first the Authority, the source from which the citation is drawn. Then I shall greet The Solidity; the quality or state of being solid. The internal coagulation or integration of the past, and my revealed purpose, await me.

THE FEMININE POWER

My soul has a voice that will be heard.

A unique voice, a voice of its own.

I am no longer afraid of that hot raging beast, this constant sensation in my stomach. It is the internal coagulation or the integration of body, soul and spirit: The coordination of the mental processes into a normal effective personality.

The operation of finding our function or I should say reason for living.

Jesus gave up everything, that we may have the honor of being the temple of His Father's Being, and know the depth of His Feminine Power or Holy

Spirit. When He took the form of humanity, He became limited, temporarily disengaged from an omnipresent power. Omnipresent – present in all places at all times. Yes, in the physical sense, He knows our infirmity, the temptations of our flesh. Why else would He leave, if for no other reason than for us to come to know the Holy Spirit personally: The Comforter had to come so the act of crucifixion would be even more glorious, the resurrection set the Comforter free to live within us. Jesus kept the form of humanity when He returned to heaven; He has memories too. Yet, the omnipresence which was taken, is now required on earth to bring comfort, peace and joy to all those who have a heart to receive.

Jesus, dying on the cross as the precious Lamb of God, slain, set mankind free from the detriment that pride and self-confidence in their works before His death brought them. By God's order He left so that the omnipresence of the Comforter could bring the assurance now desperately needed by believers. The disciples were not the only ones to need the omnipresence of a comforter.

As we allow Him through the Holy Spirit to take us through our journey of preparation for His indwelling, He through each of us is again omnipresent, which in turn will bring about divine restoration to God's world.

2 Kings 22:18-20

But to the king of Judah which sent you to enquire of the LORD, thus shall ye say to him, Thus saith the LORD God of Israel, As touching the words which thou hast heard;
Because thine heart was tender, and thou hast humbled thyself before the LORD, when thou heardest what I spake against this place, and against the inhabitants thereof, that they should become a desolation and a curse, and hast rent thy clothes, and wept before me; I also have heard thee, saith the LORD.
Behold therefore, I will gather thee unto thy fathers, and thou shalt be gathered into thy grave in peace; and thine eyes shall not see all the

evil which I will bring upon this place. And they brought the king word again.

2 Chronicles 7:14

If my people, which are called by my name, shall humble themselves, and pray, and seek my face, and turn from their wicked ways; then will I hear from heaven, and will forgive their sin, and will heal their land.

There is a reason Satan is afraid of the awakening of God's people. The enemy works relentlessly to keep us, God's chosen vessels, powerless and therefore immobile. What a battle for my soul; I am so glad that the price was paid through the Redemptive Blood, the ultimate sacrifice of Jesus' love, to release my mind to an openness for all His gifts. He gave up everything so that a nothing could become someone chosen, ordained and anointed. Oh Jesus!

Thank You sounds so insufficient. But, I do thank You and yes, I know You have not required me to become a martyr for You; I feel called, though, to offer You my life just because You gave up yours for me. I know You loved me first, but still Father, let me love You in obedience to comfort the comfortless. Take my life, Jesus, and consecrate me to Your service.

Abba Father is so fierce with anyone who grieves the Holy Spirit of Jesus. Jesus' power and authority on earth manifests itself through His saints. Only through you and I can restoration come about. Jesus loves you and me enough to trust us; in-fact, He bet His life on it.

What do I have to complain about? Why do I allow complaining to waste my time and take from me the character of Jesus Christ? I must now enter into the sanctuary of service by His authority.

Thank You, Peace Divine, for these revelations. I never did understand the real sacrifice Jesus made. Thank You for clarity. Bring to life my God-filled authority, my solidity, and my internal coagulation.

My feminine power; a potent, forceful power, full of love and compassion that will enable the feminine power in others to have life and prosper in His abundance.

Madonna Kolbenschlag writes, "Women, healed and whole, will find undreamed resources in themselves."

Sue Monk Kidd writes in, *Dance of the Desident Daughter*, as women, "If we are patient, if we are true to ourselves, if we are willing to see ourselves through the growing seasons, an inevitable thing happens. We become hearty women who have our own ground and our own understanding, sturdy as oak after the winds. We become women who let loose our strength, whose truth, creativity, and vision fly like spores into the world."

Blessed with God's anointing, my desire is that the revealing of my life that I have penned will blow with the wind, and that God's breath will take it like a blizzard of floating cotton, to cover past hurts and pain in the hearts of God's children; more importantly, though, to plant seeds of hope in the hearts of my Father's daughters all over the world for Comfort to enter in. Then the rain will come and we will shout with a single voice, "Let it rain Father; Let it rain."

Allow your truth to become a blizzard. Allow your truth to find its way through the wind, disturbing all that you believed and to gain more. Allow the blizzard to bring the life of God's Word into you, into others. The wind has the power to plant the seeds in places you will never visit personally. Plant much seed, to reap a bountiful harvest. Allow the wind to carry the seed of truth, revelation, peace, and purpose.

April 20, 2005, and it is now five minutes before the hour of two o'clock in the afternoon.

So much today.

Well, I have arrived at Sanctuary, (not that I want to sound pampered; oh well, I am pampered). I am now waiting to see what goodies Abba Father has in store for me. It's OK to ask God His plans as the Holy Spirit moves you to comfort you. I feel really great.

April 20, 2005, and it is now half-past the hour approaching four o'clock in the afternoon.

I sit with anticipation when the UPD-united parcel delivery of God rolls up in the form of my spiritual director Kathy. Oh! It's so great to see Kathy. Does she have a package for me? Did Daddy send me a gift? Thank You, Abba Father, for bringing me to this place...to know such intimacy in our relationship that I call out to You, "Daddy."

To be honest, I really wish Kathy would give me my package, and then chit chat. But no, she has to first prepare me for the delivery of my own package. Why doesn't she allow me to hold my package and then converse with me? Apparently it doesn't work that way.

"Now, let us explore a bit."

"Tell Me what are you are feeling inside?"

I want so much to say to Kathy, "I have traveled over six hours to arrive here, so what do you have for me?" But instead I shared with her what Comfort and I have talked about, how Peace Divine has introduced Herself. But I really did not know Her as yet; all the good stuff you already listened in on.

Okay, so Kathy is determined I must sign for this package first. Let me go along with her, after all I am a patient servant now. I shared with her what I felt as I drove up to the grounds of Sanctuary earlier, and I will share it with you also.

As I drove up, I felt really excited; like I had returned for something I had lost connection with. I could not have expressed these feelings previously, but in sharing with Kathy, I realized now how I felt. I was here to collect something that was taken from me – from us – long ago. The connection was somehow broken, and I am here to have it fixed.

In my heart, I sense I have come here to collect my gift sent by Daddy but wondering why won't Kathy deliver it? What is it that I am in need of? What does Kathy have? So I follow Kathy into meditation and prayer. She prayed for the light of the Holy Spirit to start at the crown of my head, and flow through my neck, my shoulders, my hands, my back, my stomach, my butt, and my feet. She then prayed for that light to expand and connect with the light on the outside of my body, that we may become one. Then she prayed her favorite prayer,

May you be at peace,

May your heart remain open,

May you awaken to the light of your own true nature,

May you be healed,

May you be a source of healing for all beings.

I have now memorized this prayer, and I don't remember ever learning the line that says; may you be healed. Did Kathy throw that line in?

"No Antoinette, she did not. These words were always a part of the prayer. You memorized that line, so now it belongs to you. You are being given the gift of healing. I am Peace Divine, but there are several aspects to my nature. You were given a gift, a present, a part of me. You were given a gift of healing."

Why do I need healing? Am I sick?

"Yes, your body, soul, and spirit were diseased. All your life you have been taking temporary measures to numb the pain, to fool the mind into thinking the body is no longer diseased. You don't have to self-medicate yourself any more, I have done the operation you were so afraid of."

Didn't You need my signed consent to perform this operation?

"Yes, and you surrendering your will to Mine gave Me consent. Also, your mother might have passed from this life; but in spite of her illness, she always prayed for you, daily. My promise to her to save her children includes you. There are also intercessors you are not aware of who constantly intercede for you."

"Do you need to know more about the consent signatures?"

No!

"The gift of healing is yours to keep."

So how do I use this gift?

"Antoinette, right now enjoy the knowledge that you have this gift."

Okay.

Finally, Kathy delivers my Daddy's gift to me. Thank you, Kathy.

The package is so beautiful, and the ribbon awesome. I don't know what's inside the package. I do not know how it will work for me, but right now I want to just hold onto my gift, and enjoy the knowledge that it belongs to me, for my use, for our use.

April 20, 2005, and it is now forty-five minutes before the hour of seven o'clock in the evening.

How do I feel about my gift?

Like someone who has being limited to using public transportation for their entire life, desiring to someday own a car, when, suddenly this person comes into possession of a car – what freedom! Unimaginable joy as a friend surprised that person with a car, a long awaited gift. It is completely wrapped and tied with large bows and the key placed in this person's hands is as striking as the vehicle itself. No confusion, just peace as they accept this wonderful gift to help them through this thoroughfare of life, including its many arteries. Where I became lost on some highway unfamiliar to me. And the rain poured down, just on me though. Didn't quite understand why or how You were able to do that, but then You are the Father Divine. I thought for awhile, I would drown until the gentleness of the Mother Divine, Your Holy Spirit, took my hand. I digressed, didn't I, but not like the pimple. Something is different now.

But back to the car: They don't know the color of the car, the make of the car, the model of the car, not even the manufacturer of the car. All they know is that they were given their dream car!

That person might even take the bus one more time to try to overcome some of the excitement of having received the desire of their heart. An overly excited daughter on the road behind the wheel of a moving car, not a very good combination. So she chooses to enjoy the knowledge of what she has received, and decides, for right now, to leave the wrapping on.

I am that excited daughter who has been given a much desired gift, but decided to leave it wrapped for now. Being too hasty could cause a fatal accident that could continue the enemy's slaughter of other souls. But hey, my gift is mine; my gift is mine. I'll tell you the color, make, model and maybe the manufacturer as I slowly, with controlled excitement, open my gift. I will definitely share with you later; some private time is in order here.

As the UPD of God was preparing to leave she asked, "Antoinette do you know what the shirt you are wearing says?" I am thinking, what I know is that I needed to get a shower and change my clothes from all that traveling before you got here. My vocal response to Kathy was, "No." She said, "Take a look."

My shirt spelled out the word "basic." Is that a coincidence or what?

Remember earlier Peace Divine instructed me to get back to basics?

Kathy said, "Well Antoinette, the message is loud and clear. Now you have 24 hours before I see you again, to learn just what basic would be for you."

As the Holy Spirit leads me, I hope to share with you later why my gift of healing arrived wrapped in a package called "back to basics" with ribbons called "obedience." Wow, even the wrapping and the ribbons I just want to enjoy. Whatever the conditions, it's fine with me. I'm loving it.

So what surprise does the wrapping and the ribbon have for me?

I am thinking...if there is a condition, there has to be a reward. I did not make up these rules. Conditions met - Rewards received. Hey! I am loving it. Are you?

April 20, 2005, and it is now fifty minutes before the hour of seven o'clock in the evening.

I sat down to eat dinner when my eyes fell on a bookcase filled with books. Walking away from the table to explore the book titles, I heard a new instruction.

"Antoinette, go back and sit down, enjoy and finish your dinner; there is indeed a time and a place for everything."

In obedience, I calmly returned to my place at the table and sat down. So my first lesson in getting back to basics, at dinner-time, I sit, eat, and enjoy. Peace Divine, please don't tell me my basic is that basic.

"Yes Antoinette, there is joy and pleasure in every area of life."

Let me get this straight; there is joy and pleasure in having dinner?

Eating food?

"Yes, Adam's first home was in a garden."

But that was a garden. All over; everywhere the eye could see – only fruits and vegetables. Where was the joy and pleasure in that?

"Antoinette, why were you called, chosen and anointed?"

So I could be used to bring about restoration.

"Right, the body was created to process only natural grains, fruits, and vegetables. Only because of the wickedness of man's heart did I allow them to consume the meat of animals, therefore shortening their lives. Now that you have become one with nature, do you still want to eat the animal who is one with you, one with nature?"

No. Peace Divine, I can see myself bonding with the chicken right about now. But the chicken, is she in Your image? Did You not give me dominion over the fowls of the air?

"With this new gift of healing, it is used to nurture and embody the sacred Feminine Divine. It will bring about fusion of the mystic and the prophet inside of you."

A mystic is one who has embraced and embodied that ultimate inner authority, and no longer depends on a source outside of herself. It usually comes about through time spent in isolation.

A prophet is one whose spiritual energy moves externally into the world.

The soul of a mystic person craves isolation from society. But that same soul has a voice. The voice of a prophet knows silence only to receive instruction. And then, in obedience the words come forth for blessing. There comes balance in total submission. The interweaving threads of the mystic and the prophet produce the conscious soul.

So, Peace Divine, with all this fusion consciousness going on, what's next?

"Antoinette, the coordination of the mental processes into a normal, effective, conscious personality. The entering of the Feminine Divine."

We will not be effective if we are only mystic in nature, or if we are only a prophet. The interweaving thread requires the fusion of both. Okay, so the gift of healing upon me is the interweaving thread used to bring about the fusion of the mystic and the prophet in me? Peace Divine, when a soul has a gift of healing, does its purpose become to share with others? Or is it that soul's personal gift?

"Antoinette, in this case, it is a gift...personal to you. There was no balance, no fusion of the mystic and the prophet in you. You are very extreme when you are being used one way or the other, but you can only be effective with the fusion of both. It is a definite requirement to become a conscious daughter."

Now, with this transforming experience I must need to find the impulse and means to express You, Peace Divine. How do I find the way to the real purpose here?

"Antoinette, you have already found the impulse and means, you are expressing it by using your experience as a testimony. As I promised you on April 8, 2005 your soul now possesses a key and I shall unlock the doors of opportunity for you in the near future, so that you may embark upon the great sea of adventure. You shall be released in a way that will most startle and amaze you."

CHAPTER NINETEEN 

Birthing: I am Home

Woke up this morning with my mind,

Stayed on Jesus.

Woke up this morning with my mind,

Stayed on Jesus.

Woke up this morning with my mind,

Stayed on Jesus.

Hal-le-luj; hal-le-luj, hallelujah.

BIRTH

So many ways to tell of what I am about,
Like all the words on this page came out of my mouth;
Or rather my heart, or spirit, or mind.
Inspired by being and the passing of time.
Well, of coming into being, being born in fact.
Like my birth years ago, how did God do that?It's amazing just to imagine, or even to think,

That first you weren't here, and then you're here in a blink.
Not really a second, more like nine months.
It didn't take long for you to develop some spunk.
First thing you do is cry to the world.
It doesn't matter what gender you are, whether boy or girl.

3Traditional gospel, Woke up This Morning

You let every one know you are here to stay.
But is that all you are saying, you're not going away?
Your entry was tough, a trying experience,
and even mom could not wait for your magnificent entrance.
So celebrate your pain, and joy wrapped together,
You'll soon see them again in a totally different order.

The experience didn't take long to usher you in time,
Don't let my thoughts stay long on your mind.
Instead think of how you got here, and how much it meant.
You were somewhere for nine months developing,
Nine months well spent. Mom sure took care of you
With all of her heart, her body also played an important part.

However it's up to you, to show what that time meant.
All locked up inside her, was it time well spent?
Show her you care for all she endured;
with you deep inside her, like fine wine been cured.
You just popped the cork and took a small peek,
Saw what you liked, and decided to leap.
Welcome to life and all that is promised.

Neil Gregson

April 21, 2005, and it is thirty minutes before seven o'clock in the morning.

An ample daylight, filled with such promise. I awoke this morning with an overwhelming feeling. I kept saying, "I am home, Jesus trusts me; He bet His life on it." Instinctively, that Jesus and I were partners in restoration haunted on this odious path; even when there was little understanding and much fear, there was this solid mass of knowing, like a conscious knowing. I would no longer have to endure double mindedness common when one is not sure of a thing. God has revealed so much to me. I raised my hand in the air for Jesus and I to shake on it. What I felt was the warm anointing of His presence flow through my hand and a wonderful joy with our communion. A re-awakening to the love He has always had for me.

Now, it seems the power to handle any situation lived in me and that power was part of His gift to me; He prepared me. Like a genius who finds no comfort in this world, disturbed by those who dare not comprehend her wealth of knowledge, I could function in this secular world, though I am no longer of this world. I am not content to be a muse to my brothers.

Created in my Father's image empowers me as His heir. Such unique creativity assigned unto me is valuable to God. My greatest passion is to see my sisters free, and sanction by their awareness of the Feminine Divine, His Holy Spirit, to comfort each of them. There is a sensation of hot burning lava in my stomach that will not be cooled until every daughter arrives into the knowledge of her freedom.

Words escape me to explain the fullness contained within the depth of my soul as I experience this feeling of power, tempered by residual rage, within me; my stomach is physically hot. I do not understand completely yet. Am I supposed to hold this growing life inside of me, or do I push it out?

Where did the word "push" come from? I sound like I am having a raging; fierce angry beast for a baby. Raging, fierce, angry, but only against the injustice and wrongful suffering of women; and yet I can feel a tenderness, a type of love in the heart of the beast, set free to nurture, protect, and enable my sisters as they come. Somebody please explain to me what I am talking about. A beast in my stomach, raging, fierce and angry? Hot lava? I am wondering if I am a baby just coming out of my mother's womb, how can I be pregnant? And pregnant with what? I really don't understand what is going on here. Mother Divine is going to be a Grandmother Divine? It's certainly time for a long walk.

> Tapping the flow of the soul is only half the creative process...the other half is figuring out how to do commerce with the practical world.
>
> Sue Monk Kidd

> Raptures and transports happen when communion is not purely spiritual. Once divine blessings are imparted straight to the Spirit, as they will be to the Perfected ones already purified by the second spiritual night, the enchantments and torments of the body cease. The soul enjoys liberation of spirit. Her senses are no longer clouded and carried away.
>
> Dark night of the soul
> Mirabai Starr

April 21, 2005, and it is thirty minutes before eleven o'clock in the morning.

There is something always before me. Have you noticed?

While here at Sanctuary, the instruction was to begin Part 3 of Raised As a Baton. I am here in my room and did not take that long walk I was planning. I just walked to the door, took some deep breaths, and have been writing and reading ever since.

The revelations received thus far are quite overwhelming, but I will not become a spiritual statistic, an overwhelmed, overexcited daughter behind the wheel of a powerful moving car. I will stay right here in this room until I am calm enough to drive. I wonder how long that will be.

I passed the required test, and after receiving my license, it seems like I only have a permit. Still, the call is for me to simply wait for the instructor. Thought I was done with him. There is a set of brakes on his side of the car.

Why the additional brakes? I do have my license, don't I? Where is he? Am I not calm enough as yet? What do you think? Am I not calm enough to be on the road? Why won't you answer me? Are there any other Divine Beings left?

Please answer me. Am I calm enough for the road?

"Antoinette, this is your brother, Lord Jesus Divine."

Lord Jesus Divine Himself? Not Abba Father God but Jesus?

"Yes this is Jesus, I am here."

Here at Sanctuary?

"Right here at Sanctuary. Remember the excitement you felt when you drove onto the grounds? You felt like you returned for something you had lost? That something was your divine connection with Me. You felt the rejoicing of your soul; your soul recognized home. The quiet, the peace, the tranquility. As your instructor, please listen. One of the aspects of My nature is that of a lamb. You described the child in your womb as a raging, fierce, angry beast."

"That might be so, but to be an effective deliverer, there has to be a fusion between the nature of the lamb (the mystic), and that of the lion (the prophet). Without the lion having a lamb-like nature, it can hurt the very cubs it was sent to save."

How are You going to fuse or entwine the nature of a lion and a lamb, which will in turn produce a mystic/prophet daughter divine?

"You will be blessed with a gift of patience, self-control, longsuffering, and love. The purification of the soul is not over. The most essential part is still to come, which is spiritual purification."

I am being given so many gifts. How old is my soul? Can my soul handle so much at once?

"Yes, that is why you are been given a gift of self-control. Your soul is 6 years old. You have grown rather rapidly. Your time of preparation is coming fast to an end. At age 7 you will have completed your time of preparation."

"At age 7, which is a symbol for completion, you will be given the key, not a gift, but the key."

What do you mean?

"You have in your possession the key of love. This key represents the authority, the solidity, and the internal coagulation of your being – The double portion or full power of the Holy Spirit. Go into the world and preach My gospel. Teach My children what I have taught you."

Comfort them?

"Yes."

"Let's work together to bring your soul to a place of calmness and control in this time of utmost excitement. You have been prepared for the night of the spirit. As a daughter chosen to ultimately merge with the Father, you must ascend to such an elevated degree of love. Many will not and most cannot reach the high levels of this process. Many daughters and sons have experienced and have successfully come through the dark night of the soul, but have not been chosen to go through the spiritual purification or night of the spirit. These, My children, are doing a most wonderful work for Me, however, many are called but few are chosen to ascend to such an elevated degree of love and will ultimately merge with Me."

Yes, yes I understand. Many are called, but few are chosen.

"The purification of the soul is not complete without the purification of the spirit. Only those of my children who have been put through both the night of the soul, and the night of the spirit, will have that unlimited, unrestricted relationship with Me. It is what I desire for all My children, but some would not be able to withstand the necessary preparation, so I allow them to serve Me in the capacity, though limited, which they have attained."

"These are My basic instructions to you, Antoinette."

"A time of meditation and breathing must become a part of your daily routine."

"I said daily."

"Daily reading of the Bible, in an atmosphere of worship."

"Set aside daily a time for prayer, reflection, thanksgiving and joy."

"Make sure you obtain your daily instructions."

"Bless someone daily. Each time you bless someone it returns to you a hundred fold."

"Meditate on what I have said; then get started."

Okay, Jesus.

"Yes."

Thank You; I love You.

"You are welcome; I love you dearly. Antoinette, you have arrived at the point of an absolute and unquestionable relationship with Me. For it seems you are ready to be poured out. You must take everything as it comes from Me. I will never guide you at some point in the future, but always here and now. The freedom you already have in Me is yours to use immediately. Use only that which you have been given. The secret to maintaining the freedom given to you in love, joy, peace, comfort, healing, and prosperity is to stay always connected with Me. My requirements are as simple as I have related them to you."

I will obey. Everything I have been through seems so extreme; and yet to maintain the restoration of my soul and its rewards seems so simple. Almost like a child could do it.

"Antoinette, not almost. Even a child could maintain the freedom and restoration once given to them. My yoke is easy and My burden is light."

Jesus, if I knew all the words to "What a mighty God we serve," I would sing it for You right now.

What a mighty God we serve,

What a mighty God we serve,

La la la la la la, oh boy!

Oh!

Angels bow before Him,

Heaven and earth adore him,

What a mighty God we serve.

Thank You so much, while I paused to listen, You reminded me of the words. Oh yes! A moment of reflection, thanksgiving and joy.

What a mighty God we serve,

What a mighty God we serve,

Angels bow before him;

Heaven and earth adore him,

What a mighty God we serve.

Oh Boy! I have to sing this song again.

What a mighty God we serve,

What a mighty God we serve,

Angels bow before him,

Heaven and earth adore him,

What a mighty God we serve.[4]

04/25/05, and it is now six thirty in the evening.

Good night, soul, I am headed for my spiritual purification. Afterwards we will have complete contemplation, ultimate merge, oneness with God.

Lord Jesus Divine, I have submitted to Your directions, prepare me for the night of the Spirit.

My intellect and senses have been purified, that has indeed freed my soul.

The soul no longer has to labor with the intellect or senses; she now finds within herself the most serene, loving contemplation and spiritual sweetness.

But the purification of the soul is not over. The essential part is still to come, which is the spiritual purification.

No matter how profound the purification of sense may have been, the purification of the soul is not complete until the spirit also is purged (Mirabai Starr).

The soul then enjoys liberation of spirit. Her senses are no longer clouded and carried away.

04/26/05, and it is now eight o'clock in the evening.

Contemplation Divine, carrier of divine light, I want to enter the illumined door, beyond which darkness is no more.

---

[4] Public Domain, Words and Music by Unverified...What a Mighty God We Serve.

I want to see the light.

I want to enter the light.

I want that ultimate merge, that lasting experience of oneness with You. Prepare my spirit and soul for that long-awaited communion with You, beyond which darkness is no more.

I am each-ness in the all-ness of God.

I acknowledge the God in me.

God is powerful.

I am powerful.

04/27/05, and it is now eight o'clock in the evening.

Even though I have submitted to the night of the spirit, there was still a dread, a deep cold dark dread present in my heart. I crawled up the stairs practically on my knees. I just needed to get to my prayer room. I felt like I was dying, but I wanted to die in the presence of the Lord. I called everyone's name that I could remember, I asked Abba Father Divine to watch over them for me.

At that point I knew I would not survive or pass any more tests. I was so tired and, yes, afraid. I did not have the strength to fight any more demons. I felt like Satan himself came to torture me; Jesus and I won, so what other demon was there for us to overcome?

I collapsed on my prayer mat thinking that this is going to be a very long night.

April 28, 2005, and it is thirty minutes before the hour of six o'clock in the evening.

I was awakened by a still small, voice.

"Antoinette, you are home. You passed the test a few days ago when you were at Sanctuary."

Oh Lord, I wasn't dead. I was fearfully dreading a major test that I had already passed. That test I chose not to share at this time. I am not sure that I can put into readable words what occurred overnight, but, upon awakening this morning a new, powerful knowledge greeted me. It's like being in a solid state of what? Solidity? It seems I had received the wrapped car, and had taken the bus one final time.

I remember last night before I fell asleep, I thought, I would choose death rather than live in fear one more day. Satan could come in any shape or form, I just knew that whether dead or alive I would be okay. My laser (car keys) would detect any and all hidden land mines set by this ruthless enemy. I jumped out of bed, laughed, and looked into the mirror. "Are You for real?"

"I am for real."

RELEASED

Now I can rest in peace
Mind is clear
Been released
Life to me is very clear.

My path is bright
With guidance from above
I'll not lose sight
Of the light of His Word and love.

Redeeming others from darkness
By His grace will I do
And sharing my life of gloom
Will hopefully bring others to you.

Use me to loose chains
Just as You freed me
Use me to ease pain
With love and care as You showed me.

Send me, Lord
To the broken woman
Send me, Lord
Help me piece in the puzzle
Destroyed by the hands of Satan
Send me, Lord
Help me lift them out of the huddle.
Send me, Lord
Send me abroad
To any who is broken
I'll adhere to Your call
Send me, Lord
To pave the way
Send me, to one and all.

Praise God! Praise God!
Through His grace
I'll stand tall
Light is here
Darkness has gone.

Oh how my heart sings with gladness!
To be free from the pit of gloom.
Betty Addison 05/17/05

CHAPTER TWENTY

Sent as a Baton: TAKING ON MY NATURE

The Joy of the Lord is my strength.

Weeping may endure for a night, but joy cometh in the morning.

(Psalm 30:5)

Oh Father Divine, another stone shaped, polished, and ready to be sent. I love You, I trust You, and I thank You. Oh wow! I am in Your heart.

"Antoinette."

Yes.

"There is yet another aspect of My nature I would love to introduce to you."

There is more?

"Yes, there is much more. Comfort, Peace, and Contemplation Divine, have prepared your soul and spirit to be ushered into the presence of Joy Divine. Joy Divine has many, many surprises in store for you."

I am sure I will recognize Joy Divine when I meet her. Oh wow!

April 29, 2005, and it is fifteen minutes before the hour of seven o'clock in the evening.

"Antoinette."

Yes, Father Divine.

"You were so joyful for the past few hours; now you are sad."

Yes, I was thinking and reflecting on my past and allowed my mind to take control of my emotions, now I can't find that thoughtless peaceful place.

"Antoinette, when you used your past experience as a witness and a testimony to bless others, you paid the final cost. Don't allow your mind to re-capture you, and take you as a prisoner. You are free from the past; you are free from the pain of the past. There is a place beyond the mind; the thoughts, that place beyond is oneness with Me. Stop talking about the past; you have passed the final test. Embrace, embrace, and embrace Joy Divine. Enjoy the now, the who you are. You haven't stopped thinking to permit Me to really show you who you are; you have listened; you have written the revelations. Good. But you have not embraced the now. It is time to embrace the now. You have been prepared to accept who you are and your purpose. Embrace yourself; the battlefield of the mind is over."

Okay.

"Joy Divine will teach you how to live always in an enlightened stage of consciousness. Your mind has grown into a monster, which can destroy you, if you allow it; but with the power of being within you, can surely conquer the mind. Look at what you have created from a place of no-mind; you are writing a book. Your creativeness emerged from a place of mental quietude; stay in that place; it is a place of peace and oneness with Me."

You are so correct; I now understand it is better when the ideas and thoughts originate from You. It's like being outside of my own limited and sometimes destructive thoughts. With You, Father Divine, my hope, my trust and my deliverance is all founded upon Your omnipotent wisdom and grace. The launching pad on which I stand is holy ground and I know it is a place where Your love lives and thrives. My struggle is not knowing how to just stop thinking my own thoughts, so I can watch and observe Your works within me.

So strange I am now craving what I thought in the past were illusions, that deeper inner place; that presence of something more genuine; something incorruptible; home. How do I become present? Become now? How do I live completely free and enlightened at all times? How do I observe the mind, instead of allowing the mind to control my emotions? I no longer desire the temporary moments of freedom and enlightenment, rather I seek the permanence of knowing holy ground. In this place, one can only stand in freedom and enlightenment. I love that place. I love the singleness with You.

I am so sad and alone whenever I allow my thoughts to stray from home.

I want to come home, and this time to stay. I am tired of running away, and then having to find my way back to You. The motels along the way don't seem so clean and welcoming any more. In fact, they all seem to have blown light bulbs and bug infestations. You know how I feel about bugs.

"Antoinette, the bugs of your mind can only remind you of the suffering and the pain of your past; they constantly attempt to crawl into your present, into your future. These bugs use your conversations, your associations, and your old habits as doorways to enter into your future; close the doors to any area of your life that provides an entrance. Do not close those doors slowly; slam them shut."

Yes, I am slamming those doors shut right now. I wish I had obeyed You years ago. This is something I already knew. Whenever I honor and accept the present, I become free from pain and suffering. It is like I am here on earth, but not of this world. I need my mind to function in this world, but I will no longer allow it to take over my life. My quest now is to keep those doors shut?

"Antoinette, always stay connected with the inner body. Do not allow any circumstance or situation to totally absorb you; always be aware of that ever-presence of the Holy Spirit. Feel her; listen to her; obey her. She will keep those doors shut, and keep you peaceful in any situation."

That feeling, the warmth, and presence comes with relationship as I mesh and dwell in the heart of your heart; the place of the heavenlies. It has been with me for so many years. I was conscious of it, but I did fully believe it was for me to know and have. For some reason I always thought I had a permanent fever; so I learned to ignore it, now I will learn how to embrace it at all times. Thank You for not leaving me even when I ignored You. I am so glad You love me first.

You loved me first and with a love so pure and unconditional.

May 8, 2005, and it is seven o'clock in the evening.

Today is Mother's day. My family made today fairly special, simple but special. How blessed I am as we spent most of the day just walking, talking, laughing, enjoying each other, and nature's beauty. I feel really great, really happy. My step-dad, who has been staying at my home for the past few months, is now preparing to return home to Antigua, West Indies. The vacuum that was then necessary for my birthing is no longer necessary. I am now safe and confident that all is well.

There is so much joy in my spirit, just knowing that all is well.

I have discovered joy in not having to worry about tomorrow.

I have discovered joy in knowing I am loved.

I have discovered joy in knowing I can truly love others.

I have discovered joy in laughing.

I have discovered joy in singing.

I have discovered joy in spending quality time with my family and friends.

I have discovered joy in watching my cat, Flexi, play.

I have discovered joy in watching the flowers as they bloom.

I have discovered joy in listening to music.

I have discovered joy in writing.

I have discovered joy in receiving the forgiveness of my Father for the sins I have committed.

I have discovered joy in the new found ability that I now possess to forgive others.

I have discovered joy in God's protection.

I have discovered joy in God's love.

I have discovered joy in the smile of God.

I have discovered joy in becoming a part of a church family.

I have discovered joy in my Father's choice of my divine purpose.

It almost seems as if Joy Divine can be found in everything that I now do. I invite You to stay with me, Joy Divine. I want always to have Your presence abide with me forever. I love You, Joy Divine.

"I love you, Antoinette."

Oh, Father, I am having so much fun! Wow!

What happens though if my world suddenly turns topsy-turvy and the storms become unrelenting again? Will I still possess Joy Divine in the midst of the storm? Will I allow this newfound joy to springboard me to the safety of my Abba Father's trusting arms and carry me through the storm? How powerful is the joy when my holy ground becomes thorny? Will I have this fun if You choose the next moment to bulldoze through my life, and all that I have and know now in the flesh becomes someone's rubbish?

"I love you, Antoinette."

CHAPTER TWENTY-ONE

Sent as a Baton: CROSSING OVER

Spiritual Bulldozer – To raze, level, demolish and clear: More plainly, a bulldozer makes the way, clears the path for others to cross over.

May 10, 2005, The Holy Spirit ministered to me, through *God's Leading Lady,* written by Bishop T. D. Jakes.

The time has come for you to step out of the shadows of your life and into the spotlight. Jesus made it clear that He came not just to free us from our failures, but that we might be free to succeed. Make no mistake. Becoming God's leading lady does not require play acting or pretending to be something you're not. On the contrary, becoming a true lady requires stripping away all the other roles and bit parts you may have settled for and acted out before. It means discovering who you are and what you are truly about, and exercising faith in your divine director, to guide you through the only authentic performance of which you are capable.

Leading lady, your time has come to quit waiting in the wings and take your place onstage. This is your cue. The time is now! You are in the race, dear lady, and you know that your legacy of greatness awaits you. You know the stakes are high. This race is for the golden, imperishable crown that your loving Creator wishes to place on you as you cross the finish line. It is the ultimate academy award, the only acknowledgement of your life's performance that matters. Discipline yourself with this higher goal in mind. Run not with uncertainty but with certainty.

Fix your eyes on the prize and do not be discouraged or discounted, no matter what obstacles may temporarily obscure your path.

Know that God Himself has chosen and ordained you as His leading lady. The show is about to begin. The curtain is going up on the next act of your life. You have everything you need to dazzle the earthly audience surrounding you and to garner the heavenly applause of He who loves you most. You are a divine diva destined for greatness, beyond what your imagination can conjure. Go out into the awaiting spotlight, dear woman, and grace the spotlight with the energy and talent that only you can pour forth.

"Have Faith."

What is Faith?

"It is the confident assurance that what we hope for is going to happen. It is the evidence of things we cannot yet see. Can you understand before your prayer, your thought, or your plans there I was I planting in your heart My will? You can only know this when your heart belongs to Me. I gave My approval to people in days of old because of their faith. By faith, understand the entire universe was formed at God's command, that what we now see did not come from anything that can be seen. There are no endings, only new beginnings."

My Commission

Isaiah 42:6-7

"I, the Lord, have called you to demonstrate my righteousness; I will guard and support you, for I have given you to my people as the personal confirmation of my covenant with them. And you will be a light to guide all nations to Me. You will open the eyes of the blind and free the captives from prison. You will release those who sit in dark dungeons. I have anointed you to bring comfort to My people. You were promised that at the end of your journey hope would be there. Antoinette, you represent hope. My child, don't lose sight of

good planning and insight. Hold unto these things tightly; for they fill you with life and bring you honor and respect. They keep you safe on your way, and keep your feet from stumbling. You can lie down without fear and enjoy pleasant dreams. You need not be afraid of disaster or the destruction that comes upon the wicked, for the Lord is your security; He will keep your foot from being caught in a trap. I am more pleased when you do what is just and right than when I am given sacrifice. Antoinette."

Yes.

"Lift up your eyes to the hills, from whence cometh your help, your help cometh from the Lord, who made heaven and earth. He will not suffer your foot to be moved. He will not slumber. Behold he that keepeth Israel shall neither slumber nor sleep. The Lord is your keeper; the Lord is your shade upon your right hand. The sun shall not smite you by day, nor the moon by night. He will not suffer your foot to be moved. He shall preserve your soul. He shall preserve your going out and your coming in from this time forth, and even forever more."

"Antoinette, you are a Spiritual Bulldozer in the Body of Christ. If you fail under pressure, your strength is not very great. Trust in the Lord with all thy heart, and lean not unto thy own understanding. In all thy ways acknowledge Him and He shall direct thy path."

I will obey You, Father Divine. I will trust You with all my heart.

CHAPTER TWENTY-TWO

Crossing Over

Jeremiah 6:16 (New International Version)

This is what the LORD says: "Stand at the crossroads and look; ask for the ancient paths, ask where the good way is, and walk in it, and you will find rest for your souls. But you said, 'We will not walk in it.'

THE YEAR OF THE SUDDENLIES
THE LAST TEARDROP

I CAN HEAR THE CRY OF MY PEOPLE.
WHERE IS GOD?
WE TRUSTED HIM.
DID HE DESERT US?
DID HE FORGET US?

As I sit and observe all that's going on around me, I wonder is Jesus really coming soon? Are we indeed the last generation? 2005, and yet one more river to cross. I know we are not a forgotten people, but are we forsaken? Among the believers of God, in a world that's more than six thousand years old, seemingly civilized, cultured and God-fearing, why is the pain of racism, injustice, hate, and betrayal so real? Where is God's presence in this land we call home? As I look into the mirror I ask myself, Am I really free? Is there freedom for my children, for us as a people?

FREEDOM: The quality or state of being free: as

(A) The absence of necessity, coercion, or constraint in choice or action.

(B) Liberation from slavery or restraints or from the power of another.

(C) Boldness of conception or execution.

Many are called as God's watchmen and watchwomen, set in place to cover and preserve a people, a nation. They are placed as God's voice, as His example.

And yet, so much hopelessness and confusion amongst those being led. The fear of God, where is it among His leaders? The anointing of God is being prostituted, sold at a price and highly devalued. His chosen children are dying, the cities crumble beneath us, as those charged to watch over our souls have fallen asleep, drunk from gulping the wine of greed, lustful for the things of this world.

Yet, I say, I believe Jesus is real and coming soon.

Yet, I say, I believe Jesus has never forsaken us as a people.

Yet, I say, I believe God's presence is here in this land we call home.

Yet, I say, I believe God has an awesome plan for this seemingly rejected people.

As I stood outside the conference room door at City Hall, in Jersey City, NJ, October 2004, I submitted myself to God, listening for His voice. He was the One who spoke. He had chosen His leader for this time. As ministers, bishops, pastors, evangelists and prophets, we followed the instructions as we were directed. We consecrated ourselves, fasting, praying and speaking of our faith as believers.

So what went wrong? November 02, 2004, the people did not elect the one we steadfastly believed God chose.

Or was he indeed elected by the people?

Where was God, and why did this happen? Satan appears to be the victor once again. Nahum 1:2-8 says,

The Lord is a jealous God, filled with vengeance and wrath. He takes revenge on all who go up against Him and furiously destroys His enemies! The Lord is slow to get angry, His power is great, and He never lets the guilty go unpunished. He displays his tremendous power; power to stir a whirlwind and cause the storm; or if He so chooses, power to calm any storm. The billowing clouds are but the dust beneath His feet. At His command oceans and rivers dry up. The lush pastures of Bashan and Carmel fade, and the green forests of Lebanon wilt. In His presence the mountains quake, snow-covered mountaintops melt away, the earth trembles, and its people are destroyed. Who dare stand before such fierce Sovereignty rooted in love for His children?

Who can survive His burning fury? His rage blazes forth like fire, and the mountains crumble to dust in His presence. The Lord is God. When trouble comes, He is the strong refuge, and He knows everyone who trusts in Him. But He sweeps away His enemies in an overwhelming flood. He pursues His foes into the darkness of night … until they turn to Him with a surging desire for His protection and love.

God has a plan; an awesome plan, and His chosen leader will indeed rise into the place of this appointed position at the accepted time.

Okay, so God has a plan; but right now there is a drowning feeling of discouragement and disappointment courted by our limited understanding of God's thoughts and ways. God did not come through again, it seems. We believed, we trusted, and yet we failed to succeed. Right now we have no further direction from God, as His silence is deafening. Only God can reveal where we go from here.

Disappointment hurts, but we do so trust You, Lord: What do we have left, but to trust in You? Keep our hope alive; keep our hearts together in unity.

Bring to pass that which You have ordained, Lord.

To see our dreams realized, our perspective has to come in line with God's. How does our point of view come in line with God's?

1. We must cultivate our capacity to view things in their true relations or relative importance.

2. We must pray for a broader perspective on the plans of God for our lives.

3. We must pray for the ability to aid and not hinder the vision of God.

Often our tiredness comes from the inward struggle, and then inescapable variance among ourselves, our families, our church, and the world. It is such a great struggle not to give up and give in to the pressures waiting to cripple and destroy us.

Chapter Twenty-Three 

Remember the Bait of Satan

I ain't gonna study war no more,
I ain't gonna study war no more.
Down by the riverside
I ain't gonna study war no more.

In the meantime, and until He comes
I say to you for Comfort's sake
Study war now.
Don't forget the bait of Satan!

Remember the bait of Satan: Yes, his lures abound waiting to steal away our hope and faith in the true and living God who upholds us.

Dear God, if only all God's children would realize the intense activity of Satan and how with such evilness in purpose he lures us with such daunting bait. From the depths of my soul, oh Lord, I cry for You to awaken Your people to the genuine bait of an enemy whose name is Satan. I cry even more that in our awakening, by obedience to Your Will, we defeat the will of this evil spirit.

"Antoinette, I remind you: 'They that wait upon the Lord shall renew their strength. They shall mount up with wings as eagles. They shall run, and not be weary, And they shall walk and not faint.'"

Often we think of the end of the journey, this journey we often call life, and we claim God's promises that at the end of our journey hope will be there. Hope is alive and is present here, right here with us, now.

The enemy's bait is called temptation, and will with great sorrow lead us to shut down our hearts, and run from God. But there is a determination, a belief, that somehow, someway this omnipresent God is not idly standing by. Our trust in Him is never fruitless, when we truly trust Him in a close and intimate relationship.

I remind you to pray, "Lead me not into temptation, but deliver me from evil.

Another weapon he uses is delusion; he engages our minds in false readings or interpretations of God's intentions, our relationship with our Creator, aberration, misunderstanding, confusion, misgivings, uncertainty and hopelessness. All these emotions push us away from believing and trusting in the only One who can lead us: Yes, I affirm this day, God will lead us. What else can we really do, but keep on believing? Obey.

On Satan's list of tried and trued weapons is isolation. When we are disappointed, a general reaction is to isolate ourselves. To separate yourself from those who love and support you through God's love is but a trap to lure you into a belief you are born to lose (so far from the truth for God's people). But, what do you do when hope dies? What do you do when you are ashamed, uncertain, and disappointed? When you have placed your heart and soul on the line, believing God for an illusive victory which leaves you feeling hurt, angered by the betrayal, and embarrassed, with no clear person or persons to whom you can direct the anger. What do you do when faced with the evilness of pride?

Yes, pride is a bait from Satan.

Your trust in God to make a way where none exists seemed fruitless. Did God not perform or was I misled in trusting Him by my personal agenda? Admittedly, we wonder now, was it His way? His plan? What does God really expect when it appears that He has failed us? What blithe defiance in our own narcissistic way presumes to think and believe the foolishness of God fails at anything? Yet, we continue to take mere baby steps, and not consistently. Yet, in our downtrodden way, we continue the way of trust, we keep on believing, we keep on hoping, and all the while we are faced with such great disappointment, rejection and abuse. But I can't help myself; I love this God Whom I do not understand.

I shall cry now and these tears will cause the rain to cease. The root deeply planted in my heart, the Elijah root, has taken hold and found its way to help me grow and find my way home. There is coming a stronger, dependable and consistent trust in my Creator, my Redeemer. The root has given me the advantage of God's view of this world, for which He Himself allowed Satan to become prince over this earth. All the testing and retesting has caused me to pour out my soul, walk away from my weak understanding and thoughtlessness of this world to trust the One whose thoughts are higher than mine, whose ways are far above mine. For as much as I don't understand, there is so much more room to trust Him and grow in His comfort that I may truly walk hand-in-hand with Comfort and comfort others.

I take off my shoes for this is Holy Ground and it is this place, filled awesomely with His presence, as I hear His voice with great clarity and know His will. In this place, I pray mightily for God to perform His will, bringing every thought and project into captivity as one who is chosen by Him.

Another bait of the enemy is impatience, as our desire for change, completion of our dreams, anxiousness to move forward in God's plan, a divinely splendid blueprint for His chosen leaders, supersedes God's order. We walk in the gifts for a brief spell, believing we are positioned at the appointed time and place to come forth by His call to perform His will. Yet, Satan's lure of material wealth causes many men and women to tragically prostitute the gifts for a price and in exchange for simple material gain. Did God make a mistake in those whom He chose? Absolutely not! There is no escaping the anointing and consequences of disobedience because God has gifted us not with just life;

rather, He bestows upon His chosen, who with a contrite and repentant spirit, seek forgiveness and then begin the real journey to know and obey the voice of God. Yes, He gives us free will and then He gives us second chances. Yes, that which Satan meant for our harm, God will, when we allow Him, use the evilness for our good and His glory (Genesis 50). Satan, no matter what his bait, will never outsmart God.

OK, so God has a plan and will raise a standard unimaginable when we consider our discouragement and disappointment.

The anointing of God is being prostituted, sold at a price for material gains. His chosen children seemingly die. Yet, we keep on trusting. We continue to believe, and yet we are still faced with such great disappointment, rejection and abuse. But, I can't help myself: I love this God even though my understanding of Him is limited.

CHAPTER TWENTY-FOUR

Self

CLARITY

There are some things in life we may not yet understand,
And even with experience, still we cannot plan.
To bring to the fore, the things hid in darkness,
And expose them with truth, and pure enlightenment.

Like the ugliness of hatred in all its fury,
How hate can influence, even determine your jury.
I mean judgment to the innocent with a verdict of guilty.
Aren't we made in God's image, peace, love and humility?

The feeling of love, overcome by hate.
Surely God couldn't be there, in such a dark place,
Without feeling or compassion, or even a care.
The world that surrounds you, they seem not to fear.

Your credo or pledge says all men are equal before God and man,
Yet for all these years, the black ones couldn't seem to stand.
You created a double standard to fool the unthinking,
who bought into your plan, and kept on in deceiving.

So many of us thought of striving to make it without preferential treatment,
Could it be possible so many minds were delinquent?
To reach the top, they would hate each other.
So many who made it, would assume your color.

Not the color on the outside, that they couldn't change,
But the one inside of them, they put in a cage.
And became a roadblock to others, all filled with rage.
Why? How could they hate themselves? By not looking back.
It's like mom said, the pot calling the kettle black.

I'm proud of who I am, and for sure of my color,
And come rain or sunshine, if I could I would choose no other.
For it's not the outside color, the one God does see,
But the color within, and just who you would be.

Be true to yourself after all is said and done,
The color out-side can't change with the sun.
But the color inside is the one that you are, and for years to come,
it will be your guiding star.

Neil Gregson 11/24/05

A brother in Christ, Pastor Diipiri Tikili from Nigeria, encouraged me. He explained the reason we become so stressed and doubtful is because self is involved. Our duty as those called and chosen by God is to walk in obedience, deliver God's message and remove ourselves. But, instead we tend to stick around for the glory. Once our assignment is accomplished, we have to remove ourselves so God can accomplish that which He set in motion.

Believe me when I say, I understand what Jonah felt when God instructed him to go to Nineveh. God sends you with a message and then He seems to change His mind, or delay the manifestation; in the flesh we view ourselves as seemingly foolish. We are given numerous harsh lessons in self and how destructive it can prove to an individual's call.

The emotions of disappointment, loss of trust and embarrassment are an overwhelming fear because once again we stand on the plate of doubt. Self-doubt.

Am I really called?

Does God speak through me?

Do I appear to be misled?

As I reflected on the past months, I relive the pain and disappointment we all felt. I stand and wonder, when will this all end? I once again live through the pain of loving and trusting a God who had again disappointed His people in the most cruel way.

Honestly, I did not understand.

I really do not understand.

I want to understand.

My people want understanding.

This pain of disappointment and defeat brought with it a gnashing painful reminder of how racism is alive and active today. Such anguish is at the spirit of racism as it refuses to go away; it just has become more subtle and sophisticated. My thoughts traveled back to the night of November 05, 2000. My family was awakened to the worst violation the soul of a family could endure. Our dignities trashed, raped, violated in a way any family; a black family should not have to endure. The pain is all too real.

On the night of November 5, 2000, I received a call from Wentworth Military Academy. What was to come would change the course of my life, the destiny and purpose of my family forever. Crossroads.

I remember well the joy we shared the day my son received and read Wentworth's welcome package. Spiritual growth is an important part of the academy's emphasis on moral instruction. The cadets were required to attend the church of their affiliation and Wentworth employs a chaplain to assist cadets individually. As well, the chaplains would lead group invocations at campus functions.

With such assurance concerning the school's commitment to the spiritual development of its students, and absorbing this wonderful opportunity, I was hardly able to contain the parental excitement of my son, the cadet. A praiseworthy wonder of God's power and direction in our lives. My family and I prayed and fasted for the ideal academy for our son. God had answered our prayers.

Yet, November 5, 2000 opened my eyes to the horror of being exposed to such injustices, particularly racial predisposition. How sad, this school, using God's name in their advertising, shook our faith with the inappropriateness of hate while failing to protect my son with fair treatment for an incident which led to an unjust prosecution. We were forced to accept a plea in a court system known for its bias against people of color, particularly as it was explained to us, "so that your family can leave this town (Lexington) alive." In fact, the attorney we paid recommended we leave the town within one hour after the court proceedings were over.

We did.

God, if You were there, why did this happen? We trusted You. You handpicked Wentworth Academy for my son Kerry to attend. Didn't You? No doubt, You opened this door.

We trusted You.

We believed and trusted You hand-picked Wentworth Academy for my son to attend. Why did You send my son to this hated place to stand falsely accused, charged and convicted by a plea that was grounded in prejudice? It is clear to me when we, as Your children, do things on our own, You don't have to finish anything we started independently of You. What is difficult, Lord, is when You don't seem to follow through when we walk in obedience and follow Your directions.

Yet, I continue to choose to trust this God.

The hope of our children is at risk as they die needlessly every day. First the spirit and then the body. Does anyone care? God, do You care? You promised that not one of our tears have fallen that You have not seen. You have seen and recorded every deed. No false accusation has gone unrecorded or is forgotten; no murderer will go unpunished. Every deed brings a reward, good or evil.

We have been robbed for far too long as a people. There are honest, hard-working, God-fearing, Holy Ghost-filled men and women amongst us: Sons and daughters who continually seek Your face. Their will is to follow Your instruction. After having done all we can do, after praying and fasting, trusting You, after standing firm on our foundation of faith in You, why so much disappointment and seemingly fruitless labor? The issues and concerns afflicting the quality of our lives are so real. So, Lord, I ask You...How long?

When shall this cloud of oppression and poverty pass for Your people? How long before we arrive to the journey's end? We are called as apostles and prophets, but are the words we preach and teach upon Your instruction, brought to manifestation? Will we look forever like fools in the eyes of the devil and his angels? In the eyes of those who arrogantly choose to dishonor You? To those who laugh and mock at the faith we continue to speak of and live our lives by? To those who say there is no God, and if there is a God, where is He? To those who mock us for still believing that You have not forgotten us?

If we were to give up faith in You, certainly we would die.

If we were to cease trusting You, yes we would perish.

To stay alive, to function, we have to hold on to a seemingly fruitless faith and trust through so much darkness, even through we have Your light leading us. So Lord, I ask, how long?

We continually claim the promises of David, that we will see the goodness of God in the land of the living. "*Then you will know that I am the Lord; those who hope in me will not be disappointed*" (Isaiah 49:23).

So Lord, I ask, how long?

Truth crushed to the ground is still truth and will rise.

Will it indeed rise?

When we state the truth, we have no responsibility to assist the truth. The truth is strong enough to stand independently because God's truth is His Word.

We, as a people, are called and chosen by God Himself. We did not choose the anointing placed on our lives, we were chosen. Take a close look at King David's life: Who would have chosen him as king after murdering so many? God did. You see, man does not see the heart, rather our outward action, reaction, appearance and color. God judges us based on the motive of our hearts and our ordained purpose. God does not allow the true nature of those called by Him to become visible to everyone until they have been prepared for service.

Let every action, every word reflect your convictions. God rewards those who accept the faith; walk and believe in His revelations. We are tested and re-tested; we have been greatly tried, but yet there is joy in knowing there is a reward.

Those chosen have been greatly abused, misjudged, hated, condemned, violated and abused as part of the training necessary for God's purpose and His reward. God permits this to prepare us for our ordained purpose and destiny in this life. In our obedience, we come to realize the awesome destiny of God's divine plan for our lives. Obedience is our golden key to prosperity.

Ahead, there are mountains, numerous clefts as we ascend into His abode and we continue to reach for new heights knowing we are on the side of God. We are part of His winning team.

Revelation is not for intellectual gratification, but for obedience. All that has happened in the past was not to our detriment, but rather God uses all things to establish a basis for the blessings beyond our imagination as we accept the responsibility of the revelation. What we fail to understand, what our ancestors, parents, and grandparents could not comprehend will come through obedience and then revelation. To whom much is given, much more is required. We step into the order of God and His order guides us, there God's plan can proceed and where there is order, tremendous and abundant blessings flow.

As a people, let us no longer mourn as victims, but instead begin to earnestly prepare ourselves to realize God has a plan; an awesome plan for good, for every son and daughter.

How will God's plan come about? In stages, day-by-day, step-by-step, prayer-by-prayer, love act by love act as we surrender our hearts to obedience: Tests to try our faith and build godly character. And when the final requirement of love breaks through to our human heart, miracles will happen. When nothing is held back; when as a people we truly care about each other; when those chosen refuse to become satisfied with being a token Black while their brothers and sisters remain oppressed and in bondage; when all is spent in loving each other; then, abuse can no longer exist. Not to itself, at least; not to anyone when we love for the sake of loving alone. This can only come about as we choose to face the truth of our past.

The truth will set us free.

The promise of a new life lies ahead.

A change.

A new beginning.

We can step into our future once we are delivered from the unresolved issues haunting us. Daunting demons hanging around to weaken us through confusion and generational curses; some perhaps bound over from the Motherland as we were ripped from our birthplace. Yes, past generations compounded by the fruit of hatred common to prejudice attempts to hold us back from realizing and walking into the divine promises for our success. We must fight for deliverance from these curses by first acknowledging they exist and believing God is for us. Just as He was for Mrs. Rosa Parks on that sunny day she absolutely refused to give up her seat to prejudice and hate, enabling millions of all races to stand up to the injustices of prejudice. Her determination dominated her fear. Yes, she was afraid, but her determination dominated her fear.

Often I wonder, why does Satan work so hard to keep us oppressed as a people? Is there a powerful force lying dormant within us? Is there something he is afraid of, that if as a people we discovered we have the weapon to destroy him and put an end to his influence?

Satan gains the victory over us when we focus on our past hurts and failures. Diversions holding us to unhealthy emotions, sick with fear, and immobile. Keeping us mentally drained and immobile is how he finds his way to the crevices of our souls; sneaking in to rob us of God's promises for our success.

The battle for leaders and children will remain fierce, but we have the victory. The battle for the soul is fought on the Mind-field and the contest is for the attention, the memory, the nerve cells, the file system of the subconscious, and ultimately for the very will of the soul. Don't pretend that hate, rejection, and injustice do not exist. Acknowledge that they do exist and allow God to bring about the long-awaited deliverance. One of our greatest errors is pretense. Pretense that we are not aware the evil does in fact still exist. The evil is practiced among believers who meet within the chambers of religion and spirituality. Pretending the evil isn't happening really slows our deliverance. We all must cross over the narrow sea of truth and reality to step into our destiny by divine purpose. Within this destiny lies everything promised by God. The body knows the truth; the spirit knows the truth; the soul needs to know the truth to step into its liberation.

I remember, as a child, I used to run away from home quite often. I recall sometimes just getting up from where I sat, walking away from my house and suddenly finding myself running, feeling as if I was being chased. Sometimes, I would stay away from home for days. Why was I running?

You see, my mom never faced the legitimacy of the fact that I was a married man's daughter. Her denial ultimately led to an unrepentant spirit. In my mind there sat this huge boulder of belief that I was unwanted, rejected, and not loved: It weighed heavily on my spirit whether true or not. My mother could not move past her denial and face the truth that would have freed us both. The facts surrounding my conception were hidden from me as a child, and as an adult I was covered by this boulder. Not until the Holy Spirit, Himself, revealed to me the source of this brokenness in my spirit, did I learn the truth.

To have confirmation of what God revealed to me as my heart opened up on these pages, I made contact with an aunt, who confirmed this revelation from the Holy Spirit. She kept saying to me there was no way I could have known, because except for her, my mother had told no one else. Continuing, she explained that during the time my mom dated my father, she was not aware of the fact that he was a married man, having migrated from Trinidad, West Indies, to Antigua, West Indies. The revelation of my father's marital status was disclosed to her only after giving birth to me. This shocking news opened the door to extreme betrayal, leading ultimately to the disease of mental illness. My mother lived and then died without realizing her deliverance this side of heaven, and never sharing with her daughter the seed of extreme betrayal planted by my earthly father.

As a people, a nation, we can realize our deliverance on this side of Heaven. Ultimately, it is truth that liberates us and brings us to a point of crossing over.

CHAPTER TWENTY-FIVE 

She's Finally Over

So glad, done got over
So glad, done got over
So glad, done got over
Done got over at last.

Who is She?
The Woman?
The Black Woman?

Questions.

How can this woman, this chosen Black woman, become aligned to receive her inheritance? This heritage, the heritage of her people?

Does she even know she has an inheritance?

Does she understand to accept she is a principal beneficiary?

As a people, let us move past the denial and begin to recognize the truth, and I repeat, recognize our truth, and begin to walk in the freedom of a new day. Break the evil soul ties historically used to destroy us. God is waiting to reveal to us our purpose as a nation, and as His chosen children. There is a window of opportunity still open to us all, but the window is fast closing.

> *And the stars of heaven fell unto the earth, even as a fig tree casteth her untimely figs, when she is shaken of a mighty wind. And the heaven departed as a scroll when it is rolled together; and every mountain and island were moved out of their places.*
>
> (Revelation 6:13-14, KJV)

Imagine Heaven departing as a scroll; imagine mountains and islands being moved out of their places; imagine containing the force of a tsunami within the confines of your soul. Breathe. Unless we are sealed and walking in the obedience of our Divine purpose, might we or shall we survive these events?

Jordan ~ the place where you begin to see beyond the natural and into the supernatural realm.

A place of peace.

A place of deep connection with God: Ongoing.

A place of singleness with the Lord,

> *For thy Maker is thy husband, Jehovah of Hosts is His name, And thy Redeemer is the Holy One of Israel, God of all the earth, He is called.*
>
> (Isaiah 54:5, YLT)

A place where there is no cause to compromise.

A place where all is real.

A place where God's mercy and peace is upon us now and all of our days.

A place where color is honored as beauty in God's sight.

A place where sons and daughters come together in love and unity.

A place we can reach only as we travel our journey individually and as a people.

A place where we will see the light.

A place where we will walk in the light...yes, a beautiful light.

A place of enlightenment, of clarity, of joy.

A place of gratitude.

A place of equality.

A place where miracles do happen.

Don't despair, where you are now is a part of the journey you must travel on your way to the future God has destined for you. Ahead of you is your inheritance of health, prosperity and favor with God and amongst men. After God has called and prepared you, no longer have you the option of being one of the guys. Stop trying to fit back into the crowd; rather stand up to this anointing which separates you and will usher you into the fullness of God's purpose for your very being. The path may become lonely, for a while, but breathe. Take in the surprises amongst the security of His presence as each day your walk becomes more personal with Him. As your relationship intensifies, His grace is omnipresent; a constant companion.

"Racism never died, it simply learned to masquerade in subtleties designed to fool the best of us. Black people are the magical faces at the bottom of society's well. Even the poorest whites, those who must live their lives only a few levels above, gain their self-esteem by gazing down on us. Surely they must know their deliverance depends on letting down their ropes. Only by working together is escape possible. Over time, many reach out but most simply watch, mesmerized into maintaining their unspoken commitment to keeping us where we are, at whatever cost to them or to us." (Derrick Bell, *Faces at the Bottom of the Well.*)

We strive to maintain the status quo, regardless of the detrimental and ultimate cost to society.

I ponder in my heart, Black people, the magical faces at the bottom of society's well. The key to the world's deliverance, and yet everything is done to keep us at the bottom. Now why is that?

We know Satan is the mastermind behind keeping the Black spirit depressed and our minds mentally disarranged and suicidal. Such concentration in keeping the Black mind at the bottom of society's well. As a natural reaction to fear, we keep a close watch on that which we fear most. So why are we so closely observed, watched, targeted, manipulated, and treated as though, if we were free, we would react like a raging beast, destroying everything in sight, or is it once freed we would deliver, bind and destroy every evil in sight?

There are two keys available: The key of love and the key of hate. Now I ponder; the ruling majority has in its possession the key of hate, the key Satan holds. What if a force, a spiritual force which in all its glory appears as a violet flame wherein lies the person of the Holy Spirit has attempted for generations to give the faces at the bottom of the well the key of love? What if this key, the means representing the true inheritance of a chosen people, symbolic of the lion of Judah, were entrusted to a woman to instigate restoration and repentance to a world, tainted by the failing of that very woman? That very black woman.

The key to this door unlocked by a woman. A Black woman.

The door locked by the key of deception, lying, envy, hate, manipulation, and false pretense. In the absence of acknowledgement, how do we begin to reconcile ourselves enveloped in insecurities except by the key of love? Ill-begotten authority, woman's power and the position of trust to unlock a door locked by God Almighty. Yes, the wonderment of God trusting a daring, Black woman on this now estranged continent of Africa where God chose to create His world and open our hearts to the power of truth and untruths. Now, this same God, does He dare to use a woman, still a Black woman, to work His forgiveness, restoration and hope into a people?

The womb of a Black woman sits at the bottom of this well in the eyes of society. Does royalty belong here? Even our Black men who lack knowledge of God as their personal Savior at times demonstrate such trepidation at the possibility of the raging beast lying dormant in the stomach of his mother, his sister, his wife, his daughter, his friend. Who will set her free?

Slap her if she gets out of line. Did I say "if"? Should have said "When," for surely she will find her voice.

The blow will remind her of who she is, or more truthfully, how devalued she has become through this immense struggle to survive.

The Black woman, who is she?

On the plantation then and the plantation now. Just a different master or more of them. Everything, every evil act imagined is done to destroy her and rape her of the dignity; this woman should have to validate her own worthiness.

If four rapes did not bring about the desired results, why stop? Why not ten to assure the murder of her spirit and soul. Kill her completely regardless of the cost. No, kill her just enough to leave behind a human receptacle, void of self-esteem, to enable those who choose to abuse her. Rape her just enough to destroy her spirit and soul.

Our eyes never leave that which we fear most.

The acts of racism and gender bias are potent; sadly, some of our Black men have fallen into these traps and have become all-too-willing vessels blinded by lust and self-centeredness.

And then there is self-hate; racism between colors masked to further cripple and hide the true purpose and destiny of the Black woman. A woman, a Black woman, a double minority. In the event being a minority doesn't become a barrier, make sure the gender thing rears its ugly head. Now, why is that? And does this distinction not separate the weight of the Black woman's crown from others?

Regardless of the racism, the abuse, the rejection, why is it almost impossible for a woman, a Black woman to hate? Is it because she holds the key, the other key? The key of love, necessary to bring about restoration. Often, the act of forgiveness comes easier for the Black woman whether she forgets the offenses or not. All she desires is to make it right. To make love reign whatever the sacrifice. There are times her sacrifice outweighs the net worth or benefit for what she gains in return for the constant wear on her soul, her spirit. What then is the final cost?

The uninformed, undisciplined Black man's first priority according to society is to make sure the Black daughters, soon to become wives, know their place in society, which is a place at the bottom of society's well. They are taught to make sure that women are devalued; that any thought of hope for a divine purpose lifting them to success is clouded by a huge question mark. Insecurity. The abuse turns her walk into one focused on simply staying alive, keeping her children alive, and this focus robs her of the vision and weakens her effort to walk boldly into her gifts. Again, why so much effort to cripple her natural, unobstructed mind development?

If, as women, Black women, we are so insignificant, weak, and mindless sex objects, then why the close watch and planned strategies to keep us conditioned and controlled? A dumb and useless dog can still thrive when ignored, abandoned emotionally and simply left alone. One may even kick that dog and she will not bite nor defend herself. At least for a while.

Do you believe as a Black woman, you are being avoided, ignored, left alone or watched endlessly? Every little detail of your existence scrutinized and criticized. Who is really the mastermind, the face, the brain behind the successful enterprises in the world? Is there a face, a hidden face, a hidden black face, a hidden Black woman's face? Does anyone know our true name, our true purpose, and our true identity? It is not just the white man or woman who does not know a Black person's name or identity, the Black person does not know either. At least until now.

Reveal to us, Lord, the Black nation's purpose, a Black woman's purpose, her true identity.

The genuine underlying reason for racism is not color, it is power.

Who was given such power originally over us? Who has it now and by what means has it been held on to?

At the conclusion of every chosen child's journey is peace, joy, wealth, prosperity, health, and favor and then comes direction: An illuminated path. God blesses and desires to return to us our inheritance. Like David, I believe as a chosen people of God we shall behold His goodness in the land of the living. We must, however, align our hearts with God's plan to receive the inheritance. Our disobedience ultimately suppresses the natural release of favor.

CHAPTER TWENTY-SIX 

Indigo

Tools to Freedom
Praise be to my God
For the tool of the Holy Spirit
This prompted me to search for light
From the dark road I have trod
With all of my might.

You gave me the tool of knowledge
Needed to know your voice
As we spoke daily
My faith grew a bit solid.

Burning with the tool of hope
I lost all fear
The tool of guidance
It even made cope.

Now with tool of trust
I know you are always there
Lord, you brought me through my worse
So, in Thee I am secure.

Your tool of love covers it all
When I could lean on no one else
Lord, you were right there when I called
You understood how I felt
When others thought I was off the wall.

I no longer see a wall

No longer in darkness
For Jesus took it all
Turned that darkness into success.

No turning back
I'm singing and jumping with joy
For there is nothing I lack
My Lord will not bestow.

Now I am prepared to use my tools
And go where God demands
As He directs my feet and hands
I'll care for and serve every man.

Betty Addison, 05/17/05

So this is not my story, but really represents the life and journey of my people...the original Israel. We are not the color black as we have been taught for one cannot see black. Rather, the color indigo, the base for all colors. The societal conditioning of being black brought with it a stigma of evil, bad, unworthy, and inherent attitudes ultimately leading to the justification by whites as well those of darker hue, a devaluing of our human-ness.

On the continent of Africa, Adam and Eve were thrust into the Garden of Eden to live out their lives. Logically, one would imagine the color of the skin to have a darker pigment to withstand the incredible heat generated by the sun's rays. What happens to a person's skin if that person spends time in the sun, or visits a tanning salon? Naturally, the skin gravitates to its original color; it's that simple.

Indigo is the base for all colors. The core of the earth. Indigo represents light and truth; the higher power calls it the element of the earth, the intelligence of the earth. Black is invisible to the naked eye: So, who is black and how is that person seen?

How difficult it is for Jesus to watch His brothers and sisters raped, sold, abused, killed all the day long, pushed into a corner of invisibility, even being told they are the color Black and accepting invisibility. My God.

What exactly happened to the records of my people in Lexington, Missouri? What did Jim Crow and his followers take from us? I wonder who is really the mastermind behind the writings of Jim Crow. Who would have been given such wisdom, a gift of wisdom, the knowledge needed to psychologically hold captive the mind, the black mind, the black woman's mind, for hundreds of generations? Were we betrayed; extremely betrayed. The Holy Spirit for first-hand evidence led my family there. Evidence of what? The first shall be last and the last first.

Speak, Father.

<u>May 22, 2005</u>, and it is thirty-nine minutes past the hour of one o'clock in the afternoon.

This is mind-boggling.

I returned to Sanctuary in Beallsville, Maryland to attend a planned retreat (The Light and Living Series, directed and coordinated by the Reverend Norma Jennings ... Author of *Touchstones to Remembering Your Spirit*). Now, recall at the end, Sub-title "Restoration," I shared a story about my son and I being lost in a strange village. The only person who shared the truth with us about finding our way home was an old lady. Well, that lady's spirit became a familiar spirit once I met my new teacher, the Reverend Norma Jennings. This spirit is alive and very real. Her spirit, that of a spiritual guide, is not just a dream, but alive and active in the service of the Lord. I met this spirit who guided me over one year ago in a dream. That spirit is clothed in the person of Reverend Norma Jennings. From May 20 to May 22, 2005, I sat in her presence. It was not until the seminar ended, and we all had gone our separate ways, that the revelation of who this spirit was became known to me. If only I had known, I would have asked her a lot more questions. I can only imagine how happy she was that I did not know or had recognized her.

Exactly one month following the gift of healing at Sanctuary, I was handed *Touchstones to Remembering Your Spirit* written, but more importantly lived, by this wonderful woman of God. The perfect accompaniment to alignment.

Previously, I told you I would let you know the color, make, model and maybe manufacturer of the vehicle I used in an analogy. Well, the color is indigo (no surprise here); the make is human; the model is woman herself, and the manufacturer is of course Almighty God, Himself.

Beneath all the wrapping, a woman, a stilled but exciting Black woman, the color of indigo. The woman entrusted with the principles to find our way home.

CHAPTER TWENTY-SEVEN 

The Black Woman...This Woman of Color

RESURRECTION

Alone in the still dark of night.
Silent; nothing; not even a breeze.
Just me and the thoughts about my life.
Like death, and misery, and pain, and fright.
Thinking, searching my mind to find an escape,
Some place to run to for safety and light.

To see the sun rise, and feel the wind blow,
Making a new start, and even to get up and go.
Go nowhere, somewhere, anywhere, but here.
Maybe even feel alive, and some joy inside.
Not fearing living any more, my night has disappeared.

To a bright sunny day, with a clear blue sky,
I am no longer alone, because now I can fly.
Way up above the clouds, into the wild blue yonder,
Where dreams come true, and there is no more wonder.
To experience such bliss is unbelievable.
I finally escaped the darkness, it was so unbearable.

I want to pinch myself, or even to shout,
At the top of my lungs, to make sure that I'm out.
That I am not dreaming, and it's about to be over,
So that I can stay in the wild blue yonder.
I feel like living again, and now even more.
I know that my life is a gift, I will finally soar.

Way up in the sky where dreams do come true,
Where there is no more darkness, or ever feeling blue.
Or ever alone, and never in despair,
Because I am resurrected, and my life is in repair.
To feel whole and to give to the world,
This wonderful gift of love, it's about to unfurl.

Neil Gregson

She has been tested.

She has been tried.

She overcame, she survived.

Each phase of her life,

Each season of her journey.

Tested, tried, yet she survived.

Who is she?

Why take her life? All she did was survive (almost died trying).

She is called, ordained, and chosen to lead a nation, a dying nation; a dying black nation; to lead a chosen people home. She is the caretaker of all God's children and not begrudgingly. She is the voice of justice in a land void of all fear of God…an unwise land. She is the one chosen to voice God's dissent and love. She represents hope.

The inheritance of God's chosen people shall return to them because of her. Because she chose life, a nation, a chosen people shall live. The restoration of all things? She is the baton anointed by the Holy Spirit to bring about restoration of all things. Tested? Oh yes, tested. (Tired, but still filled with the joy of her Lord.) Tested in life's three major challenges; her sexuality, finances, and hunger; hunger for the truth. Her love for her Father far exceeded all the challenges God allowed her to travail through because He loved her first.

The abuse of her people always seemed to have a right to enter and to force itself upon them. They could never quite protect themselves as if they had no rights.

God, the Father, shall overturn the captivity of Israel. The captivity of a chosen people. His chosen children.

What has been the captivity of a nation called and chosen? Rejection, abandonment, and insecurity. Yet, God the Father shall overturn the captivity of those, all those He has chosen. They shall no longer experience rejection, abandonment or insecurity. They shall know freedom to worship God, the God of their fathers, Abraham, Isaac and Jacob. They shall see the goodness of the Lord in the land of the living. Oppression is lifted now, and removed from them through revelation of truth. No longer shall memories of the past smother a people; boggle them and bind them in the pain of their widowhood. The shame of our youth is behind us and God's chosen, beautiful women, beautiful black women, are established in the love of His righteousness; they shall be far from oppression; fear, nor terror shall no longer come near them. Hallelujah!

And then, at the end of the journey, and the end shall surely come, hope awaits us; hope has carried us to this river. We have crossed the last river, accompanied by hope and with the blessedness of God's timing; His order.

June 10, 2005...12 o'clock midnight to 5 o'clock in the morning.

Severe war of the mind at Sanctuary.

I don't quite understand what happened, but suddenly there came this intense war for my mind. Again, Jesus and I won. A nation will live because I chose life. Our Father's prodigal children are coming back home to Him. Our Father Divine is revealing our inheritance. Our deliverance has come, the Titanic in our souls having being removed. The blessings we realize here are but a shadow of the rewards to come. Eyes have not seen, nor ears heard, the things and plans God has prepared for His chosen children.

Satan can only confuse the process, not stop it; he could not change the end results of our Father's plan for us. God's chosen have gone through not merely the dark night of the soul, but also the night of the spirit. They shall ascend to such an elevated degree of love and will in due course merge with their Father.

The joy of the Lord is our strength.

Weeping may endure for a night, but joy cometh in the morning (Psalm 30.5). In this moment, I dance with my Father. I dance His song of joy.

God has sent the light to draw all nations to Him. The flickering, but steady gleam of His light shines brightly across all religious boundaries, from this time forth and even forever more. From this time forth and even forever more.

And now, my friend, that boulder pressed into your spirit, God removes it!

No more tears, no more sorrows!

Extreme betrayal requires extreme forgiveness, lest the bitterness shall burn holes in your soul. The bitterness in the absence of forgiveness will cause the very core of your soul to fester. Freedom is a spiritual journey and it is not merely about destination but more about the process in the present moment. The object and design of our existence is joy, and we will only find this joy in the intimacy of relationship with God Almighty. We exercise the joy with obedience, reflecting His love.

Addendum

Author: Jay Brinkmeyer

For I am not ashamed of the gospel of Christ: for it is the power of God unto salvation to everyone that believes.

(Romans 1:16)

PUSH!

For I am not ashamed of the gospel of Christ: for it is the power of God unto salvation to everyone that believes.

(Romans 1:16)

A man was sleeping at night in his cabin when suddenly his room filled with light and an Angel appeared. The Angel of the Lord told the man He had work for him to do, and showed him a large rock in front of his cabin. The Angel explained that the man was to push against the rock with all his might. This, the man did, day after day.

For many years he toiled from sunup to sundown, his shoulder set squarely against the cold, massive surface of the unmoving rock, pushing with all his might. Each night the man returned to his cabin sore, and worn out, feeling that his whole day had been spent in vain.

Seeing that the man was showing signs of discouragement, an Evil Spirit decided to enter the picture by placing thoughts into the man's weary mind: "You have been pushing against that rock for a long time, and it hasn't budged. Why kill yourself over this? You are never going to move it." Thus giving the man the impression that the task was impossible and that he was a failure.

These thoughts discouraged and disheartened the man. "Why kill myself over this?" he thought. "I'll just put in my time, giving just the minimum effort and that will be good enough."

And that is what he planned to do until one day he decided to make it a matter of prayer and take his troubled thoughts to the Lord. "Lord," he said, "I have labored long and hard in Your service, putting all my strength to do that which You have asked. Yet, after all this time, I have not even budged that rock by half a millimeter. What is wrong? Why am I failing?"

The Lord returned to the man and responded compassionately, "My friend, when I asked you to serve Me and you accepted, I told you that your task was to push against the rock with all your strength, which you have done. Never once did I mention to you that I expected you to move it. Your task was to push. And now you come to Me, with your strength spent, thinking that you have failed. But, is that really so?"

"Look at yourself. Your arms are strong and muscled, your back sinewy and brown, your hands are callused from constant pressure, and your legs have become massive and hard. Through opposition you have grown much and your abilities now surpass that which you used to have. Yet you haven't moved the rock. But your calling was to be obedient and to push and to exercise your faith and trust in My wisdom. This you have done. I, My friend, will now move the rock."

At times, when we hear a word from God, we tend to use our own intellect to decipher what He wants, when actually what God wants is just simple obedience and faith in Him. Have you been pushing against a rock recently, trying to help a friend by yourself, wrestling with troubling finances, or trying to find a direction for your life?

By all means, exercise the faith that moves mountains, but know that it is still God who moves the mountains. Blessings on your faith walk.

THE STONE THAT THE BUILDER REFUSED HAS BECOME THE TOP CORNERSTONE.

Printed in the United States
91496LV00003B/103-201/A

9 781593 522520